Non-Accidental Head Injury
in Young Children

Non-Accidental Head Injury
in Young Children

Medical, Legal and Social Responses

Cathy Cobley and Tom Sanders

Jessica Kingsley Publishers
London and Philadelphia

First published in 2007
by Jessica Kingsley Publishers
116 Pentonville Road
London N1 9JB, UK
and
400 Market Street, Suite 400
Philadelphia, PA 19106, USA

www.jkp.com

Library of Congress Cataloging in Publication Data

Cobley, Cathy.
  Non-accidental head injury in young children : medical, legal and
social responses / Cathy Cobley and Tom Sanders ; foreword by The
Rt. Hon. Lord Justice Wall.
     p. ; cm.
  Includes bibliographical references and index.
  ISBN-13: 978-1-84310-360-8 (alk. paper)
  ISBN-10: 1-84310-360-5 (alk. paper)
  1. Shaken baby syndrome--Great Britain. 2. Shaken baby syndrome
--Law and legislation--Great Britain.   I. Sanders, Tom, 1968-   .
II. Title.
  [DNLM: 1. Child Abuse--legislation & jurisprudence--Great Britain.
2. Child--Great Britain. 3. Craniocerebral Trauma--Great Britain.
4. Shaken Baby Syndrome--Great Britain.   WA 33 FA1 C656n 2007]
RJ375.C63 2007
617.10083--dc22

                                                     2006033262

British Library Cataloguing in Publication Data
A CIP catalogue record for this book is available from the British Library

ISBN-13: 978 1 84310 360 8
ISBN-10: 1 84310 360 5

Printed and bound in Great Britain by
Athenaeum Press, Gateshead, Tyne and Wear

Contents

List of figures

List of tables

Foreword

For all the disciplines engaged in the practice and study of both family law and the criminal law, non-accidental head injuries in young children pose some of the greatest difficulties and give rise to the most rigorous challenges. It is a subject on which there remains a divergence of responsible medical opinion; where the symptomatology is itself controversial; where it is very difficult to be certain of the timing of the injuries and the number of incidents involved; and in which the interpretation of scans (whether CT or MRI) requires highly specialist expertise. Add to that already complex cocktail the fact that perpetrators rarely if ever give a true account of what has occurred, and the difficulties of establishing precisely what has happened to the injured child are self-evident. Yet few areas of child abuse have more significant long term consequences for the children involved – that is, of course, where they survive.

The minefields in the forensic context are legion, and in the criminal context have had far-reaching consequences. Even in the family justice system, where proceedings involving non-accidental head injury are rigorously examined by a specialist judiciary, care proceedings in which all the professionals in every discipline are of unimpeachable competence can still carry the danger of a miscarriage of justice, as in *W v Oldham* MBC [2006] 1 FLR 543, a decision of the civil division of the Court of Appeal which, rightly, has not escaped the authors' notice.

Against that background, I welcome this user-friendly book, which not only provides a helpful and balanced *tour d'horizon*, but also puts the subject both in its historical context and in the context of the authors' own well-focused and interesting research.

Child abuse, of which non-accidental head injury is a significant element, is an all-too-prevalent social evil. To combat it effectively, we must understand it. This book is a useful contribution to that process, and I commend it to readers from all the disciplines engaged in the criminal and family justice systems.

The Rt. Hon. Lord Justice Wall

Introduction

We hope that this book will attract readers from a wide variety of disciplines who wish to gain an insight into the challenges faced in responding to cases of non-accidental head injury in young children. As an aid to clarity, by way of introduction we address three issues: first, we provide an explanation of the relationship between non-accidental head injury and shaken baby syndrome in order to justify what, at first sight, may appear to be our interchangeable use of the terms throughout the book; second, as many readers will not have a medical background, we explain the key medical terms and associated phrases which we use and, finally, we outline the background and rationale of the empirical research we have conducted in this area and explain how we have incorporated the research findings into our analysis and critique of current issues at various stages in the book.

What's in a name? Shaken baby syndrome and non-accidental head injury

As the title indicates, the central focus of this book is on non-accidental head injury (NAHI) in young children. However, as will soon be evident to the reader, we frequently make reference to 'shaken baby syndrome' (SBS). As we explain in detail in Chapter 2, SBS has traditionally been used to explain a constellation of injuries in a young child which typically include subdural haemorrhages, retinal haemorrhages and encephalopathy and which are thought to have been caused by violent shaking of the child. To many the terms NAHI and SBS appear synonymous and indeed, SBS has frequently been used as a generic term for NAHI. However, this has the potential to lead to confusion as it implies shaking as the cause of all NAHI. As we explain in Chapter 2, the current controversy over the cause of the injuries in cases of alleged SBS has resulted in a preference for the more objective term NAHI, which does not infer any specific mechanism of the injury or injuries. In the light of recent events we have restricted our use of the term SBS to those sections of the book in which we are specifically referring to the phenomenon of the syndrome as traditionally understood. In all other contexts, we adopt the more neutral term of NAHI.

Explanation of terminology and abbreviations used

Apnoea: temporary cessation of breathing.

Diffuse axonal injury (DAI): widespread injury to the delicate axonal nerves of the brain, whereby they are stretched and/or torn.

Encephalopathy: an abnormal condition of the structure or function of the brain.

Hypoxia: a lack of oxygen in the tissues.

Non-accidental injury (NAI): injury caused to a child, either intentionally, recklessly or negligently.

Non-accidental head injury (NAHI): non-accidental injury inflicted to a child's head.

Retinal haemorrhage (RH): bleeding within the retina, which is the light sensitive layer that lines the interior of the eye.

Shaken baby syndrome (SBS): a constellation of clinical findings in a young child believed to have been caused by shaking. The clinical findings variously include: subdural haemorrhages, retinal haemorrhages, encephalopathy and multiple fractures in the long bones (and ribs).

Subdural haemorrhage (SDH): bleeding into the area between the dura mater (the outer membrane which covers the brain and lines the skull) and the arachnoid mater (the middle membrane that covers the brain).

The triad: the three intracranial injuries, the finding of which in young children has traditionally been considered to the hallmark of shaken baby syndrome. The injuries consist of subdural haemorrhages, retinal haemorrhages and encephalopathy.

The role of our research findings

The first population based case series study of infants who had sustained a SDH was published in the UK in 1998 (Jayawant *et al.* 1998). This study revealed important details on the epidemiology, associated features and investigation of SDH, which is often the first clinical sign to be picked up on a computerised tomography (CT) or magnetic resonance imaging (MRI) scan or at post mortem that alerts the paediatrician to a likely diagnosis of

NAHI. The study suggested that, in the absence of alternative explanations, many clinicians were not eliminating the possibility of child abuse in their diagnostic work in all cases. However, although the study indicated that there were shortcomings in the evidence available on which to base subsequent decisions, it provided no detail on the social and legal decision-making process and outcomes. Our research project, which was funded by the Nuffield Foundation, was therefore designed to investigate the quantity and quality of evidence recorded when a SDH is detected and during subsequent investigations, and to evaluate the use made of such evidence in the decision-making processes which determine the social and legal consequences for the victims and their families. An overview of the research methodology and results can be found in the appendix to this book.

The research project was completed in 2002. However since that time, significant developments have taken place in this area, including new scientific research on the causes of head trauma in children and the detailed scrutiny of the evidence provided by medical expert witnesses in legal proceedings. We have watched events unfold with interest. This book combines an analysis of our research evidence with a policy critique of the current medical, legal and social responses to NAHI in young children in the light of more recent events. We believe that this approach will give the reader a unique insight into the challenges faced in responding to these difficult cases. We hope that the book will be useful to a wide range of practitioners and that it will also make a significant contribution to the academic debate in a rapidly developing and frequently controversial area.

CHAPTER 1

The Problem of Child Abuse: Recognition, Responses and Re-evaluations

We begin this chapter with a historical overview of the process of recognition of child abuse as a significant social problem requiring a structured framework for state intervention in family life. We consider the key developments in social and political activity since the mid twentieth century which culminated in the Children Act 1989. The 1989 Act has been described as the most comprehensive and radical piece of legislation relating to children, and this Act, together with the Working Together guidance on the arrangements for inter-agency co-operation for the protection of children from abuse published in 1991, formed the legal and practical frameworks for responding to suspicions of child abuse during the 1990s, when the cases of suspected non-accidental head injury (NAHI) in our research cohort were investigated. We then examine the increasing emphasis being placed on safeguarding and promoting the welfare of all children in need in the late 1990s which led to the revision of the Working Together guidance in 1999, before moving on to developments in the twenty-first century, exploring reactions to Lord Laming's inquiry into the death of Victoria Climbié and the resulting changes brought about by the Children Act 2004. We consider how the new frameworks for intervention currently being structured are likely to impact on society's response to cases of suspected or known abuse. We conclude the chapter by considering the extent of the problem of physical child abuse in England and Wales, with particular reference to the abuse of babies and very young children.

The process of recognition of child abuse

The phenomenon of child abuse is not new – children have undoubtedly been abused in one way or another since time immemorial. Yet it is only in comparatively recent times that we, as a society, have been prepared to recognise the fact that child abuse is a significant social problem and to respond by developing legal and practical frameworks for dealing with cases of suspected and proven abuse. It has been suggested that a community comes to recognise the existence of the abuse of children in a sequence of developing stages, as shown in Figure 1.1.

Stage 1	Widespread denial that either physical or sexual abuse exists to a significant extent.
Stage 2	The 'battered child' is recognised. The community begins to find ways of coping more effectively with physical abuse through early recognition and intervention.
Stage 3	Physical abuse is better handled. More attention is focused on child neglect and more subtle forms of abuse.
Stage 4	The community recognises emotional abuse as a social problem.
Stage 5	The community pays attention to the serious plight of the sexually abused child.
Stage 6	The guarantee that each child is truly wanted and provided with loving care, decent shelter and food, and first class preventive and curative care.

Figure 1.1: The process of recognition of child abuse (CIBA Foundation 1984)

Whilst such stages are useful in that they are illustrative of how society has gradually come to recognise the various forms of child abuse over a period of time, in reality they are something of a blunt instrument and it would be misleading to treat the stages as distinct steps in the process of recognition. Perceptions of child abuse vary, not only across time, but also between professions and throughout society as a whole. The divisions between each stage may be blurred and at any one time different professions may well be at different stages, with public awareness frequently following a long way behind. Furthermore, there are inevitably sub-categories within each category of abuse – physical, emotional, sexual and neglect – and recognition of such sub-categories may well be subject to different time scales. For example, although physical abuse was the first category of child abuse to be generally recognised, Munchausen's syndrome by proxy (illness in children which is fabricated or induced) was only recognised as a form of physical abuse in the 1990s and it was not until 2002 that specific guidance on this form of abuse was published (Department of Health *et al.* 2002). Similarly, in Chapter 2 we explore the process of recognition of NAHI in young children and the creation of shaken baby syndrome (SBS) during the late twentieth century as a sub-category of physical abuse. However, with these caveats in mind, the stages in Figure 1.1 serve a useful purpose in illustrating the process of recognition and, by way of introduction, in the following section we chart the process in relation to all forms of child abuse from the late nineteenth century to the present day, identifying, in general terms, the first five stages.

Child cruelty first gained explicit recognition at the end of the nineteenth century. Initial recognition of the abused and neglected child has traditionally been attributed to events in the USA, although, in fact, attention had first been drawn to the problem in France in the mid nineteenth century (Tardieu 1860). The Society for the Prevention of Cruelty to Children (SPCC) was first founded in America in 1871. Five years earlier, the American Society for the Prevention of Cruelty to Animals (ASPCA) had been formed and it was to this society that appeals were made to intervene when the case of a little girl who was beaten daily by her stepmother came to light. The existing law offered the child no protection until the guilt of the mother had been established and it was only through the efforts of the ASPCA, who succeeded in persuading a court to interpret the word 'animal' to include a child, that the girl was saved. Recognition that the law accorded more protection to animals than it did to children led to the foundation of the SPCC (Cobley 1995). Within five years ten more such societies had been formed. News of the American experience reached the UK and the first such society was founded in Britain in 1882. Other societies followed and eventually merged to form the National Society for the Prevention of Cruelty to Children (NSPCC) which was granted its Royal Charter in 1894. The NSPCC, together with the National Vigilance Association, were successful in highlighting the problem of child abuse and the lack of an adequate legal response. In 1889, Parliament enacted the Prevention of Cruelty Act. For the first time child cruelty and neglect were made statutory criminal offences and the Act gave the police and the courts powers to intervene in cases where ill-treatment was suspected and to remove children from their parents where necessary. The discovery of X-rays in 1895 also provided instruments to assist in diagnosing physical abuse. Further legislation followed, including the Punishment of Incest Act 1908, which for the first time made incest a criminal, as opposed to an ecclesiastical, offence. At the same time, the Children Act of 1908 established juvenile courts as a separate forum with jurisdiction over both abused and neglected children and delinquent juveniles. Therefore, by the beginning of the twentieth century, society had developed a rudimentary framework for dealing with cases of child abuse, which included provisions of criminal law to punish abusers and laws authorising the withdrawal of parental authority or custody over children at risk.

However, the subject of child abuse remained shrouded in secrecy for many years. Concerns were voiced periodically throughout the early part of the twentieth century and in 1950 guidelines were issued dealing with children ill-treated in their own homes (Home Office, Ministry of Health and Ministry of Education 1950). Yet at this time child abuse was not generally regarded as a significant social problem. Both the general public and professionals seemed to have great difficulty accepting the possibility that adults maltreated or sexually abused children. When presented with a child with injuries, clinicians often failed to connect the injuries with child abuse, either because the possibility did not occur to them, or because they were not psychologically prepared to believe that adults, and in particular parents, could commit such atrocities on a child. No criticism can be attributed to clinicians for this at this time – they were merely reflecting existing social norms. Even if clinicians did recognise the possibility of abuse, in stark contrast to the current position, they were provided with no formal guidance on the action to be taken and, in the absence of a planned strategy of state intervention, were left unsure of their responsibilities.

The 1960s saw the creation of the 'battered baby syndrome'. In 1962, in an article in the Journal of the American Medical Association, Henry Kempe, an American paediatrician, and his associates put the unthinkable into words: some of the physical injuries of children were not caused by accidents at all, they asserted, but were in fact the result of physical assaults by adults on children (Kempe *et al.* 1962). The battered baby syndrome came into being, the problem was forced out into the open and public opinion began to change. Kempe himself has admitted that he used shock tactics in an effort to increase recognition of the problem of physical abuse. During a lecture to the British Association of Paediatricians in 1970 he said:

> I was so exasperated by my colleagues' lack of attention that I deliberately used the words 'battered baby syndrome' because they were provocative enough to arouse anger. Indeed, for ten years previously I had spoken of child abuse, non-accidental injury or inflicted

wounds, but few people paid any attention. I therefore wanted to provoke the emotional reaction and shock which more moderate and scientifically more satisfactory terms had not provoked. (European Committee on Crime Problems 1981, p.20)

Kempe's shock tactics worked in America. By 1967, all American states had enacted child abuse reporting laws which made the reporting of suspected child abuse mandatory for certain professionals. Although such a system of mandatory reporting has never been enacted in the UK, public awareness of the problem of physical child abuse increased tremendously during the 1960s and 1970s, partly, it seems, as a result of the American experience.

During the 1970s attention also began to be focused on the emotionally abused child. All abuse inevitably involves some emotional ill-treatment, but it came to be realised that there were various types of behaviour by an adult which were emotionally harmful to a child, even in the absence of physical or sexual abuse or neglect, and emotional abuse was first introduced as a criterion for inclusion on child protection registers in 1980 (Department of Health 1980). Although the scars of emotional abuse may be less obvious, at the beginning of the 1980s it was thought to be more common than the combined total of physical and sexual abuse (Oates 1982, p.3) and today registrations on the child protection registers under the category of emotional abuse remain the second largest category, exceeded only by registrations for neglect (Department for Education and Skills 2006a). The 1980s also saw an increasing recognition of sexual abuse, which culminated in the events in Cleveland in 1987. The resulting inquiry (Butler Sloss 1988) and national media coverage ensured that the issue of child sexual abuse was pushed to the fore. Thus as a society we have moved through a process of recognising various forms of child abuse, clearly reaching stage 5 in Figure 1.1. Many hoped that the advent of the Children Act 1989, within which there are provisions for children in need and for the support and help of families, signalled arrival at stage 6 of the process. Sadly, subsequent events, many of which we discuss in this and subsequent chapters of the book, have proved only too vividly that this is not the case.

Child protection: the legislative background

Although a rudimentary framework for dealing with cases of child abuse was in existence by the beginning of the twentieth century, the emergence of philanthropic societies to rescue children from neglectful parents and cruel environments allowed the state to play a nominal but authoritative role in child protection (Parton 1985). During the twentieth century the role of the state in protecting children was gradually strengthened, with the Children and Young Persons Act 1933 imposing a duty on local education authorities to investigate and prosecute parents or guardians who neglected their children. The period following the Second World War corresponded with the development of social intervention and the establishment of the welfare state and, in keeping with this ethos, the Children Act 1948 established local authority children's departments under the supervision of the Home Office. The 1948 Act initiated a child care service which tried to help those children whose homes had failed them but which also emphasised the restoration of children in care to their natural parents. During the second half of the twentieth century a more sophisticated framework began to emerge. The Children and Young Persons Act 1963 imposed a duty on local authorities to promote the welfare of children by working with families to prevent children coming into care.

However, it was the death of Maria Colwell, who died at the hands of her stepfather in 1973 despite a multitude of agencies being involved and the resulting government inquiry into her death (Inquiry Report 1974), which is said to have signalled the beginning of modern political, public and professional interest in child abuse and led to fundamental changes in policy and practice (Parton 1991). The inquiry report into Maria's death criticised the child care system for its failure to protect Maria, and also implicitly criticised the underlying policies, especially the emphasis given by child care workers to maintaining the 'natural' family through their adherence to the 'blood-tie'. The Children Act 1975, which followed the inquiry report, was firmly rooted in state paternalism and stressed children's need for permanency, even if this was in substitute families (Daniel and Ivatts 1998). The 1980s have been described as a decade during which the long-established tensions between child care policy, parental responsibility and rights, and the jurisdiction of the state finally snapped (Hendrick 2005, p.47). The problem was generally perceived as one of a lack of proper balance between too much and too little intervention by social workers and increasingly calls were made for a new partnership between parents and the state. The Children Act 1989 was introduced as a way of re-establishing an appropriate balance in the child protection system via a new legislative framework (Parton 2005).

The legal framework of child protection: the Children Act 1989

The Children Act 1989 was implemented in England and Wales on 14 October 1991 and, despite significant changes to the implementation of its provisions in practice (discussed below), the legal framework to protect children contained within the Act remains in force today. The Act reflects new thinking on the relationship between parents and their children by encouraging co-operation and partnership between families and the agencies charged with the duty of safeguarding and promoting the welfare of children. The aim of the Act is to provide an effective legal framework for the protection of children and, in so doing, it enshrines five main principles: the child's welfare is the paramount consideration; children are best cared for by both parents wherever possible; the state and courts should intervene only where it will make improvements for the child; delay is not generally in the best interests of the child; and the laws and procedures regarding children should be unified.

The first of these principles had been enshrined in child care legislation for some considerable time. References to a child's welfare are to be found in the Guardianship of Minors Act 1886 and by 1925 the Guardianship of Infants Act of that year provided that, in deciding issues concerning the custody or upbringing of a child, all courts were to regard the child's welfare as the first and paramount consideration. (The change in wording from 'first and paramount consideration' to 'paramount consideration' was not intended to lead to a change in the law.) The second principle underlying the Act is based on the belief that children are generally best looked after by both parents playing an active role and without resort to legal proceedings. Section 17 of the Act imposes a general duty on local authorities to safeguard and promote the welfare of children in their areas who are 'in need' and, so far as is consistent with that duty, to promote the upbringing of such children by their families by providing a range and level of services appropriate to those children's needs. Children in need are defined as those whose vulnerability is such that they are unlikely to reach or maintain a satisfactory level of health or development, or whose health or development will be significantly impaired without the provision of services, plus those who are disabled. Abused children and those at risk of abuse are therefore children in need. In addition to the duty to provide services to these children, parts IV and V of the Act provide the legal framework for the care, supervision and protection of abused children and those at risk of abuse. The third principle of non-intervention requires a court to be satisfied that any order it makes will make a positive contribution to the welfare of the child, thus helping to avoid unnecessary state intervention and preserve the integrity and independence of the family (s 1(5)) and the fourth principle requires a court to have regard to the general principle that any delay in determining a question with respect to a child's upbringing is likely to prejudice the welfare of the child (s 1(2)). The final principle is implemented by the creation of a three-tiered court comprising the High Court, county court and magistrates' court (family proceedings court), each with concurrent jurisdiction under the Act enabling cases to be transferred up, down and across the system subject to specified criteria.

One of the main changes brought about by the 1989 Act was the introduction of a uniform threshold criterion, below which state intervention in family life would not be justified. Prior to the implementation of the Act, the grounds for state intervention in a child's life were diverse. A child could be taken into the care of the local authority by a number of different routes and the conditions determining whether such compulsory measures could be taken varied according to the route by which each case progressed. The threshold criterion adopted by the 1989 Act is that of 'significant harm', and all provisions within the legal framework of child protection require reasonable suspicion, reasonable belief or proof that the child concerned is suffering or is likely to suffer significant harm. We consider these provisions and the concept of proof in detail in Chapter 4.

As we shall see, the twenty-first century has seen radical changes to the structures and responsibilities of agencies concerned with the welfare of children, yet the legal framework to protect children contained within the 1989 Act has survived virtually intact. However, although Laming (2003) found that the legal framework was basically sound and the introduction of the threshold criterion of significant harm has generally been seen as a significant improvement on the pre-existing law, the principles underlying the 1989 Act have not escaped criticism, and questions have been raised as to whether the Act succeeded in establishing an appropriate balance between too little and too much intervention. In a damning indictment of the workings of the Act, Speight and Wynne (2000a) claimed that the balance was weighted too firmly in favour of non-intervention and claimed that the Act was failing severely abused and neglected children. In particular, Speight and Wynne referred to the 'resurgence of the blood link ideology' (p.193) and questioned the principle that children are generally best looked after within the family. They pointed out that, whilst this principle would be unexceptional as a general aim for an ideal society in which child abuse and neglect did not exist, in the real world it was debatable and they questioned the existence of evidence that abused and neglected children are best returned to abusing and neglectful parents. Furthermore, they claimed that the principle that the child's welfare is paramount is not an effective counterbalance, as the Act states that in general children should be kept in their natural families, thereby effectively creating a closed loop.

In response Lady Justice Hale, who was the Law Commissioner in charge of the programme of reform in family law from 1984 to 1993 and was also a member of the interdepartmental review of child care law published in 1985 which led to the 1989 Act, expressed sadness and concern at the criticisms (Hale 2000). She pointed out that Speight and Wynne may have forgotten that the Act was concerned with *all* children, and not just the abused and neglected, and that one of the Act's main aims was to integrate all the law relating to the upbringing of children, including disabled children. Hale was of the view that any civilised society had to start from the proposition that children were best brought up in their own families as it was the bedrock of society that children belong in families and not to the state. Hale concluded her response by saying 'It is us, not the Act, who are to blame if seriously abused children are not receiving the protection they deserve' – a statement which was prophetic of the conclusions reached by Lord Laming two years later following his inquiry into the death of Victoria Climbié.

In a counter-response, Speight and Wynne (2000b) accepted some of the points made by Hale and strongly endorsed her concluding remarks. However, they stood by their assertion that an unqualified statement that children are generally best looked after within the family was 'positively dangerous' in an Act that deals with abuse and neglect. Entering the debate, Harrison, Masson and Spencer (2001) pointed out that article 8 of the European Convention on Human Rights, which was incorporated into domestic law from 2 October 2000 by the Human Rights Act 1998, requires respect for family life and allows intervention only where it is legally endorsed and to the extent necessary to protect the welfare of the child. Case law in the European Court of Human Rights has upheld the principle that child care interventions should be limited and focused on family reunification and Harrison *et al.* claimed that the law and practice in the 1980s which preceded the 1989 Act was unacceptable by these standards. Finding, and maintaining, the appropriate balance between too little and too much intervention is no doubt one of the most challenging tasks in ensuring an effective system of child protection. The legal framework provided by the 1989 Act at least provides the tools for this task – the 'fine tuning' of the balance is left to the way in which these tools are used in practice.

The practical framework of child protection: inter-agency co-operation

Whilst the 1989 Act clearly places primary responsibility for investigating concerns that a child may be suffering significant harm on local authorities (s 47(1)), it makes it clear that they are not expected to investigate alone and the Act also imposes a duty on a range of other authorities to assist local authorities with their inquiries if called upon to do so, unless it would be unreasonable in all the circumstances of the case (s 47(9)). The relevant authorities include any other local authority, any local education authority, any local housing authority, any Health Authority, Special Health Authority, Primary Care Trust, National Health Service (NHS) trust or NHS foundation trust. A recognition that inter-agency co-operation is required to deal with cases of suspected child abuse was, of course, not new to the 1989 Act. As long ago as 1950 a government circular on the ill-treatment of children recommended the establishment of Children's Co-ordinating Committees and by the early 1970s inter-agency co-operation had become commonplace (Hallet and Stevenson 1980). More formalised structures to facilitate inter-agency co-operation were put in place in 1974 in the wake of the Maria Colwell inquiry. These included the formation of Area Review Committees (subsequently designated Area Child Protection Committees), the holding of case conferences (subsequently designated child protection conferences) in every case involving suspected non-accidental injury (NAI) and the establishment of a child protection register. As Parton (1991) points out, the current system of child abuse management was effectively inaugurated at this time. By 2003 Lyon et al. (2003) noted that much had been adapted, improved and revised (p.232) and further reform has since been made by the Children Act 2004 (see below), but the underlying ethos of inter-agency co-operation remains the central component in the management of child abuse today.

Inter-agency co-operation 1991–1999: Working Together under the Children Act 1989 to protect children from abuse
Whilst a statutory duty to co-operate is imposed by the 1989 Act itself, those involved are provided with detailed guidance as to the arrangements for inter-agency co-operation – commonly referred to as 'Working Together'. The guidance is issued under s 7 of the Local Authority Social Services Act 1970 and does not have the full force of statute. Nevertheless, it is expected that the guidance will be complied with 'unless local circumstances indicate exceptional reasons which justify a variation'. The initial guidance was published in 1988, before the implementation of the 1989 Act (Department of Health and the Welsh Office 1988). Following the implementation of the 1989 Act, revised guidance was issued in 1991 (Home Office *et al.* 1991). Between 1988 and 1991, the guidance had grown from 72 pages to 126 pages in length, arguably indicative not only of the increasing significance being attached to inter-agency co-operation, but also the increasing complexities of the guidance with which practitioners were expected to comply. As the title indicates, the focus of the guidance at this time was clearly the protection of children from abuse. The 1991 version of Working Together was the governing guidance during the investigation of the cases in our research cohort and, in discussing the research findings, we have tried to highlight any relevant changes made in the subsequent revisions to the guidance which were published after the cases in the research cohort had been investigated.

Changing the balance: inter-agency co-operation from 1999: Working Together to safeguard and promote the welfare of children
In 1995 the Department of Health published a series of research projects into the functioning of the child protection system, together with an overview summary (Department of Health 1995) which concluded that there was a bias in practice towards assessment rather than prevention and treatment and that too much of the work undertaken by social workers came under the banner of 'child protection'. The research showed that some professionals were using s 47 inquiries inappropriately as a passport to services for children in need, but that over half of the 160,000 or so children who were subject to child protection inquiries received no further services once the inquiry had been completed. The report encouraged local authorities to reconsider the balance of services and called for an approach that

encouraged a perspective on cases as children in need even where there may be a protection problem. As Reder and Duncan (2004) point out, while there was never an overt instruction for social services to refocus their work away from investigation, it was common knowledge that they understood that this was expected of them and as a result, referred cases were increasingly dichotomised from the outset, based on limited information, as being either a 'child in need' (therefore requiring supportive services) or 'child protection' (hence requiring an assessment).

The findings of the research projects led the government to encourage agencies to take a more balanced approach to the provision of services for children in need and in 1998 a consultation exercise on the creation of new guidance for inter-agency co-operation was undertaken, one of the stated aims of which was to promote a new emphasis on looking more widely at the needs of the most vulnerable children and families (Department of Health 1998). The resulting third revisions to the Working Together guidance were published in 1999 for England and 2000 for Wales (Department of Health, Home Office and Department for Education and Employment 1999; National Assembly for Wales 2000). (Following the enactment of the Government of Wales Act on 1 July 1999, the National Assembly for Wales assumed responsibility for health and social services in Wales. However, the systems for child protection in Wales closely follow those in England and in subsequent discussion we assume the same systems apply in each country, unless otherwise indicated.) These guidelines clearly set responsibility for the protection of children from abuse as a subset within a wider responsibility to safeguard and promote the welfare of children and they were accompanied by the publication of a framework for the assessment of children in need and their families (Department of Health 2000), which social services were encouraged to adopt for all children in need, including those where there were concerns that a child might be suffering significant harm.

The change in focus from protecting children from abuse to safeguarding and promoting their welfare has clear implications for a child who may be at risk of abuse, where the dichotomy between a child in need of services and a child in need of protection may well be blurred and the approach adopted at the outset may determine the final outcome for the child. However, it may be thought that a child presenting with physical injuries indicative of possible NAI would automatically be categorised under the umbrella of 'child protection' and thus the change would not impact on children who have been abused in the same way as it impacts on those at risk of abuse. Certainly, we have no evidence to suggest that the categorisation and initial investigation of the cases in our research cohort would have been markedly different *solely* as a result of the change in focus following the 1999 guidelines (as opposed to changes attributable to the increased awareness of NAHI and the growing expertise in the investigation of cases during the 1990s discussed in following chapters). Yet the move towards a more holistic approach to vulnerable children and their families clearly has the potential to impact on decisions taken following an initial investigation where there remains a suspicion of abuse. For example, at the time the cases in our research cohort were investigated, the decision to place a child's name on the child protection register was generally based on a retrospective review of the evidence that triggered the child protection referral, whereas following the 1999 guidance and the assessment framework, the decision focused on a prospective assessment of the likelihood of continuing risk of significant harm. These changes have led to a marked decrease in the number of children on child protection registers overall so that between March 1999 and March 2005 the number of children registered in England fell from 31,900 to 25,900 (Department for Education and Skills 2006a). However, we can only speculate on the impact of such changes on the decision to place a child's name on the register in cases of NAHI (Cobley and Sanders 2003). Furthermore, at this moment in time we can only speculate on the likely impact of further, more radical changes implemented in the wake of the tragic death of Victoria Climbié.

A new framework for the twenty-first century: ensuring Every Child Matters

In 1974 the inquiry into the death of Maria Colwell became a catalyst for changing professional practice and promoting inter-agency working which resulted in the development of a child protection system, the basis of which remained in force for over 30 years. Failures in the system were all too commonplace during this period and between 1973 and 2000 there were at least 80 inquiries into the deaths or serious abuse of children who were known to, or involved with, agencies who had a duty to safeguard their well-being (Corby 2003). However, it was the death of Victoria Climbié in February 2000 which became the catalyst for the most recent radical overhaul of children's services. At eight years of age Victoria died from hypothermia, malnutrition and physical abuse at the hands of her carers, her great-aunt and her cohabitee. Her great-aunt had brought Victoria from the

Ivory Coast, initially to France and then to London, supposedly in search of a better life and education for her. During the last ten months of her life, Victoria had been known to four local authority social service departments, three housing authorities and two police child protection teams. She had been referred to a specialist family centre managed by the NSPCC and was admitted with suspected non-accidental injuries to the paediatric wards of two different hospitals within the space of ten days.

Lord Laming was appointed to conduct an inquiry into the circumstances leading to and surrounding Victoria's death (Laming 2003) and the inquiry found that, between April 1999 and February 2000, the relevant services had the opportunity to intervene to protect Victoria on 12 occasions, but they failed to do so. As the inquiry report concluded, the failure to protect Victoria was 'lamentable'. However, Victoria was found to have died because those responsible for her care adopted poor practice standards and the inquiry report concluded that the legal framework for child protection set out in the Children Act 1989 was basically sound. The resulting overhaul of children's services therefore focuses on the practical implementation of the legal framework and the delivery of services. The Children Act 1989 functions of social services remain unchanged, but the way in which they are delivered at local level is set to change radically.

Lord Laming's inquiry report was published in January 2003 and contained 108 recommendations. By June of that year the government had issued new practice guidance (Department of Health *et al.* 2003) which summarised the key processes of interagency co-operation and was intended as a shorter, 'user-friendly' version of the full Working Together guidance published in 1999. In September 2003, two key documents were published: a detailed response to the practice recommendations made by Lord Laming (Department for Education and Skills, Department of Health and Home Office 2003) and the Green Paper 'Every Child Matters' (Department for Education and Skills 2003). The Green Paper set out the government's wider strategy to reform children's services and formed the basis of a change for children programme which aimed to put in place a national framework to support the joining up of services so that every child could achieve the five key outcomes identified in the paper: being healthy; staying safe; enjoying and achieving; making a positive contribution; and economic well-being. Where statutory reform was necessary to achieve these objectives, the relevant measures were enacted in the Children Act 2004. The Act imposes a duty on local authorities in England and Wales to make arrangements to promote co-operation between agencies in order to improve children's well-being (defined by reference to the five key outcomes identified in the Green Paper) and also imposes a duty on key partners to take part in those arrangements.

Specified agencies who work with children are now required to put in place arrangements to make sure they take account of the need to safeguard and promote the welfare of children when doing their jobs. A Common Assessment Framework (CAF) has been developed as a nationally standardised approach to conducting an assessment of the needs of children and deciding how those needs should be met and all local authorities are expected to implement the CAF by the end of 2008. From April 2006, Area Child Protection Committees are replaced by Local Safeguarding Children Boards set up by local authorities and key partners are required to take part in these Boards. In the light of these new duties and responsibilities imposed on agencies to safeguard and promote the welfare of children, a plethora of guidance has been issued, including a revised edition of the Working Together to Safeguard Children guidance (Department for Education and Skills 2005a, b, c, d; Department for Education and Skills 2006b).

Following the recommendation of Lord Laming that the government should actively explore the benefit to children of setting up a national database on all children under the age of 16, the 2004 Act also makes provision for the setting up of databases that contain basic information about children to help professionals in working together to provide early support for children and their families. The initial proposal was to develop a database that would contain the details of every child in the UK which could be accessed by child protection professionals, including social workers, police officers and medical professionals and would effectively provide a national child protection register. It was envisaged that staff would be able to record notes about a child and flag up any concerns they may have. However, doubts were voiced over the confidentiality of the information contained on any such database and experts warned that the cost of developing such a system could run into hundreds of millions of pounds and that the system would be swamped with concern warnings. Despite such doubts and warnings, the government decided to move forward on the development of a database. During 2005 a series of trailblazer projects took place across England.

The results convinced the government that an Information Sharing Index could be developed in which children, young people and parents would have confidence and which would help local authorities and a wide range of children's services practitioners to do their jobs more effectively and provide better services. During 2006, further development and building of the technical solution are planned, together with data trials to test the accuracy of existing data sources. It is envisaged that there will be one central Index in England containing basic information on all children up to the age of 18 years. The data will be partitioned into 150 parts, one relating to each local authority in England. Local authorities will be responsible for maintaining the accuracy of data for children in their area, for controlling user access and maintaining security, and for training staff to use the Index correctly. Central government will fund both the initial implementation costs (estimated at £224 million over three years) and the operating costs (estimated at £41 million per annum). Testing and piloting of the index is scheduled to start in 2007 with roll-out completed during 2008 (Department for Education and Skills 2005e).

These changes continue the trend, which started in the 1990s, of placing increasing emphasis on safeguarding and promoting the welfare of all children. As Parton (2004) notes, it is apparent that in recent years the responsibilities of local authority social services departments have both broadened considerably and intensified. While at any one time there will only be a small minority of children in a local authority who will be on the formal caseloads of a social worker, and an even smaller number who will be on either a child protection register or in the care of the local authority, the responsibilities of local authorities are now very wide indeed and in effect include all children in their areas. Whilst the burden is shared to some extent, as agencies with which local authorities work have also found their responsibilities broadened, the challenges posed for the newly configured children's services should not be underestimated. If the services can rise to the challenge, in theory, the reforms should lead us towards the utopia of stage 6 in Figure 1.1 – the guaranteeing that each child is truly wanted and provided with loving care, decent shelter and food, and first class preventive and curative care. However, in practice, efforts must be made to ensure that attention and resources are not inappropriately diverted away from front-line child protection work. As we have noted, the last 15 years have seen a discernible shift towards treating the protection of children from abuse as a subset of a far wider responsibility to safeguard and promote the welfare of all children. Care now needs to be taken to ensure that the subset does not become completely subsumed within this wider responsibility in which the protection of children from abuse no longer exists as an objective in its own right.

Child abuse: the extent of the problem

Reliable epidemiological data on the nature and extent of child abuse is crucial to the development of sound public health and social welfare policies, intervention programmes and prevention strategies. However, the number of cases of child abuse has been likened to an iceberg (European Committee on Crime Problems 1981) which can be divided into different levels, as indicated in Figure 1.2. At the base of the iceberg, cases of abuse at levels 5 and 4 are unreported and will not form part of any official statistics. Even where official statistics are available on cases at levels 3 to 1, they do not necessarily provide a complete picture, as discussed below, and thus determining the true extent of child abuse is a process fraught with difficulties.

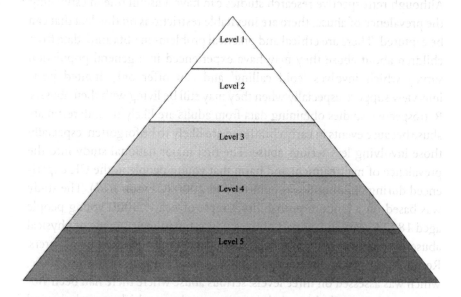

Level 1: Those children whose abuse is recorded in the criminal statistics.

Level 2: Those children who are officially recorded as being in need of protection (i.e. those recorded on a child protection register).

Level 3: Those children who have been reported to child protection agencies or other professionals, such as teachers or clinicians, but who have not been registered.

Level 4: Abused children who are recognised as such by relatives, but who are not reported to any professional agency.

Level 5: Those children who have not been recognised as abused by anyone, except (perhaps) the victim and/or abuser.

Figure 1.2: The iceberg of child abuse (Creighton 2004)

Despite such difficulties, attempts can be made to estimate the prevalence (the proportion of a defined population who have been abused during a specified time period) and incidence (the number of new cases occurring in a defined population over a year) of child abuse in England and Wales by a variety of methods. We review these methods below with the aim of providing an overall picture of the extent of physical abuse against children, before moving on to focus on the extent of abuse of babies and very young children, with particular reference to NAHI.

Measuring the entire iceberg of abuse: the use of retrospective research studies

Although retrospective research studies can have a useful role in estimating the prevalence of abuse, there are inevitable restrictions on the data that can be captured. There are ethical and practical problems in obtaining data from children about abuse they may have experienced in a general population survey which involves 'cold calling' and can offer only limited post-interview support, especially when they may still be living with their abusers. Retrospective studies obtaining data from adults are likely to underestimate abuse because events in early childhood are likely to be forgotten, especially those involving less serious abuse. The first major national study into the prevalence of maltreatment and harm that young people in the UK experienced during childhood was published in 2000 (Cawson *et al.*). The study was based on a random probability sample of nearly 3000 young people aged 18–24 years and, as part of the study, estimation was made of physical abuse by parents, including step-parents and other quasi-parental carers. Responses were combined into a comprehensive measure of physical abuse, which was assessed on three levels: serious abuse where there had been violent treatment regularly over the years, or violence which caused physical injury or frequently led to physical effects lasting at least one day; intermediate abuse where either violent treatment occurred irregularly and with less frequent lasting physical effects, or where other physical treatment/discipline such as slaps, smacks and pinches occurred regularly and caused injury or regularly had lasting physical effects; and cause for concern, where less serious physical treatment/discipline occurred regularly, or where irregular physical discipline often had lasting effects.

Using these definitions, the study found that 7 per cent of the sample was assessed as seriously physically abused at the hands of their parents or carers, 14 per cent as experiencing intermediate abuse and 3 per cent as cause for concern. As the child population for the UK is approximately 12 million, the 7 per cent of the sample who were assessed as having been seriously abused represents 840,000 children. When the estimates for other forms of abuse are taken into account, it has been estimated that 16 per cent of children experienced serious maltreatment by their parents during their childhood, of whom one third experienced more than one type of abuse (Cawson 2002). This represents nearly a million children who have been subjected to serious maltreatment during their childhood.

Measuring reported abuse: child protection statistics

In 2005, 552,000 referrals were made to social services departments in England (Department for Education and Skills 2006a). However, whilst this figure undoubtedly includes many abused children and those at risk of abuse, it also includes other children whose needs are not related to the threat of ill-treatment, and the published statistics make no distinction between the two. A clearer picture can be gleaned from statistics relating to s 47 inquiries and child protection registers. In the year to 31 March 2005, an estimated 68,500 children (62 per 10,000 children under 18 years) were the subject of s 47 inquiries in England, of whom 37,400 (34 per 10,000 children under 18 years) were the subject of an initial child protection conference during the year. Following the initial child protection conference, 30,700 children were registered on a child protection register. At 31 March 2005, there were a total of 25,900 children on child protection registers in England, representing a rate of 23 children per 10,000 population aged under 18. Eighteen per cent of these were registered under the category of physical abuse. However, the registers only contain the names of children who have been identified by the authorities as being in need of a child protection plan and they do not contain a complete list of all the children in the area who have experienced or are likely to experience significant harm. They are not therefore a measure of the incidence of abuse, although they do give some indication of the scale of the problem.

The actual number of children on child protection registers in Wales is, of course, significantly smaller due to the size of the population, but the proportion of children on child protection registers is significantly higher. At 31 March 2005, there were 2269 children registered, representing a rate of 35 children per 10,000 population aged under 18 years. Of these 425 were registered under the category of physical abuse, although concerns about physical abuse combined with neglect and sexual abuse were recorded in a further 161 cases (National Assembly for Wales 2005).

The tip of the iceberg: criminal statistics

An alternative source of data can be found in the criminal statistics for England and Wales, which provide details on the number of offenders cautioned or convicted of specified criminal offences. However, the statistics will only show cases at level 1 at the very tip of the iceberg. Furthermore, the statistics are generally categorised by offence and offender – not by victim. Therefore, unless the offence is one in which the age of the victim is an integral part, the statistics will give no indication of this. In cases of physical abuse where the child survives, the only relevant statistics are those relating to cautions and convictions for the offence of cruelty to or neglect of children under s 1 of the Children and Young Persons Act 1933, although no distinction is made between physical cruelty and neglect. In 1994 430 offenders were found guilty or cautioned of this offence. A decade later in 2004 this figure had risen to 1218 offenders, which still only represents the very tip of the iceberg. Where a child has died as a result of abuse, the statistics show that the average annual number of child homicides (which include both murder and manslaughter) is 79, which provides substantiation for the NSPCC statement that on average one or two children are killed every week (Creighton and Tissier 2003).

The abuse of very young children

The statistics show that babies under one represent a major group on child protection registers, being more than twice as likely to be registered in England than the 'all children average'. Based on registration figures, babies under one are more vulnerable to all forms of abuse, especially physical abuse and neglect (Breslin and Evans 2004). More detailed research has been undertaken on the incidence of physical child abuse in Wales between 1996 and 1998. In a population-based incidence study, using a capture-recapture analysis on data obtained from the Welsh Paediatric Surveillance Unit and child protection registers in Wales, Sibert et al. (2002) found an incidence of all physical abuse in babies under one year of age of 114 babies per 100,000 population, representing 1 in 880 babies abused in the first year of life. As Sibert et al. point out, these figures are broadly in line with earlier studies in the UK which found incidence rates of 85 per 100,000

(Kempe 1971) and 100 per 100,000 (Baldwin and Oliver 1975), although research in the US found a much lower figure of 31 per 100,000 children (Ards and Harrell 1993).

The research by Sibert *et al.* (2002) also investigated the incidence of severe physical abuse in children under the age of 14 years. (Severe physical abuse was defined as that which was consistent with grievous bodily harm in a criminal law context, which we discuss in more detail in Chapter 4.) The research found that severe abuse was six times more common in babies under one year (54 children per 100,000 population) than in children one year to four years of age (9.2 children per 100,000 population) and 120 times more common than in five to 13-year-olds (0.47 children per 100,000 population). The particular vulnerability of very young children to abuse is, of course, not unique to England and Wales. A study on the incidence of reported child abuse and neglect in Canada (excluding Quebec) in 2003 found that while the incidence of substantiated maltreatment in all children up to 15 years of age was 21.71 children per 1000 population, the incidence in babies under one year was 28.15 children per 1000 population (Trocmé *et al.* 2005). Although the incidence of maltreatment is only about a third higher in babies (suggesting a significantly smaller discrepancy than that found in the UK), the Canadian statistics include all forms of child maltreatment. We know that babies are more vulnerable to physical abuse than to other kinds of maltreatment and physical abuse forms less than a quarter of substantiated maltreatment in Canada (5.31 children per 1000 population), which suggests that there is probably a significantly greater distinction in cases of physical abuse in Canada than the published figures show.

'Babies incubated in terror'

The level of physical abuse inflicted on very young children is obviously a cause for grave concern, particularly when the abuse leads to the child's death or leaves the child with long-term disability, as we discuss below in relation to the infliction of NAHI. However, the physical effect of any injuries resulting from abuse is only one aspect of the impact of abuse. It is commonly assumed that, in the absence of physical scars or disabilities, very young children will have little or no memory of abuse in infancy and therefore will not be affected *psychologically* by abuse in the early years of their life. However, in the growing field of research into infant brain development, studies have shown that the structure of the developing infant brain is susceptible to *physiological* damage, independent of any damage caused by the abuse itself, which may impact on future behaviour patterns. Perry (1995) has found that traumatic experiences in the early months and years of an infant's life elevate levels of stress hormones, such as cortisol, which have a toxic effect on an infant's brain. For example, an infant growing up in an atmosphere of unpredictable violence is likely to become hyper-vigilant to perceptions of threat. For such a child the slightest stress unleashes a new surge of stress hormones, making the child over-prepared to respond impulsively and aggressively (Department for Education and Skills 2004a). As a result, Hosking and Walsh (2005) suggest that a propensity to violence develops primarily from wrong treatment before the age of three years. Trauma experienced by very young children is also said to scramble neurotransmitter signals that play key roles in telling growing brain cells where to go and what to connect to, leaving children exposed to chronic and unpredictable stress with deficits in their ability to learn. As Hosking and Walsh (2005) conclude, 'babies brought up in violent families are incubated in terror and their brains can be permanently damaged' (p.19). Thus the impact of abuse of very young children extends well beyond any physical injuries inflicted and may well make a significant contribution to the growing cycle of violence in today's society.

Non-accidental head injury

Very young children have been found to be particularly vulnerable to two types of physical injury: subdural haemorrhages (SDH) and fractures. The research by Sibert et al. (2002) estimated an annual incidence of brain injury and SDH of 34 children per 100,000 population in babies under six months and 8.5 children per 100,000 population in babies aged six months to one year. (The corresponding incidence rates for fractures were 56.8 and 39.8 children per 100,000 population.) Sibert et al.'s estimated incidence of brain injury and SDH in babies is in line with the findings of previous studies. The first population based case series of infants who had suffered a SDH was published in the UK in 1998 (Jayawant et al. 1998). The study identified 33 cases of SDH in children under two years of age in South Wales and south west England between January 1993 and December 1995, giving an estimated annual incidence of 12.8 children per 100,000 population in children under two years of age, rising to 21 children per 100,000 population in babies under the age of one year. Eighty-two per cent of the cases studied had factors highly suggestive of abuse, such as unrecognised fractures, burns and a previous history of abuse within the family. Two years later a prospective population based study of paediatric units in Scotland during 1998–9 was published, which found an annual incidence of 24.6 children per 100,000 population in babies younger than one year (Barlow and Minns 2000). When the estimated annual incidence of NAHI in babies less than one year old is combined with Sibert *et al.*'s estimated incidence of all physical abuse in babies of the same age, approximately 20 per cent of abused babies suffer NAHI.

The implications of this for policy and practice should not be underestimated. Research has shown that there is a significant mortality rate amongst infants who sustain a SDH as a result of abuse and survivors have serious morbidity and special education needs. The study by Jayawant *et al.* (1998) found that the prognosis in such cases is poor – of the 33 cases ascertained, 9 children died (27%) and 15 (45%) sustained significant disability. In our research 14 of the 68 children in the cohort died – a mortality rate of 25 per cent (Cobley and Sanders 2003) and studies in the USA have reported mortality rates of up to 50 per cent (Starling, Holden and Jenny 1995). Research by Barlow, Thomson and Minns (1999) found that 78 per cent of survivors had significant long-term neurological and developmental abnormalities. Karandikar *et al.* (2004) studied 65 children under the age of two years who had suffered NAHI and SDH. Sixteen of the children died (24.6%) and of the 45 children followed up for a period between 21.7 and 103 months, 25 had a good outcome, 6 were moderately disabled, 11 were severely disabled and 3 were in a persistent vegetative state. The problems identified included cerebral palsy (16 children), ongoing seizures (5 children), visual problems (11 children), speech and language problems (17 children) and behavioural problems (13 children).

Although we cannot measure the actual extent of child abuse there can be no doubt that, as a society, we at least now recognise that it is a significant problem and we are doing our best to find the most appropriate way in which to respond. There is a growing body of evidence to show that babies and very young children are particularly vulnerable to physical abuse, that NAHI is commonly inflicted on these children, and that the effects of such injuries can be devastating, not only for the child and his or her immediate family, but for society as a whole. In the following chapters we explore the medical, legal and social responses to cases of suspected NAHI in young children in detail.

CHAPTER 2

Constructing and Deconstructing Shaken Baby Syndrome: Changing Cultural Definitions and Medical Practice

In this chapter we trace the historical development of shaken baby syndrome (SBS) from its inception in the 1970s to the present day. The scientific basis of the syndrome has become the object of criticism and the generic phrase 'non-accidental head injury' (NAHI) is increasingly being used in preference to the term SBS to describe the constellation of injuries commonly associated with the syndrome. The question that we consider is how SBS has been constructed and what attempts have been made in recent times, particularly by the medical profession, to deconstruct it and unravel the causal mechanism which has recently generated increasing controversy. This is a legitimate question as recent medical controversies surrounding the likely cause of the syndrome have raised doubts about the proposition that only shaking can explain the clinical signs. Initially, we address the question of how SBS has been defined historically and describe the rapidly changing social and scientific context in which the syndrome is currently defined and conceptualised. In so doing we examine the construction of SBS in relation to some of the debates in scientific medicine. We conclude the chapter with an examination of the medical control or 'medicalisation' of SBS by showing how medicine has sought to re-conceptualise a social phenomenon as a biomedical construct. We illustrate the danger of conceptualising behavioural problems using a strictly medical definition, and assess whether the increased public mistrust of medicine is undermining medicine's ability to offer adequate scientific explanations for complex injuries in young children.

Shaken baby syndrome: historical development of a medical phenomenon

SBS is a phenomenon that has attracted widespread media attention in recent years, partly because of the dramatic nature of the injuries incurred by young children and the disputed nature of clinical science in this area of child health. However, historically, NAHI in children, and more specifically SBS, have received limited attention in the media as well as within medicine as a legitimate field of scientific inquiry. This is predominantly because NAI was not a primary concern for scientific medicine prior to the Second World War, but was perceived widely as a priority area for child protection agencies such as social work and the police. Until the late nineteenth century, child maltreatment was not recognised as a medical issue and received limited public attention. During this period, even if abuse was recognised, abused children were typically brought to police and social service agencies, sometimes receiving the benefit of a doctor's opinion, although clinicians did not play the leadership role that they play today (Evans 2004).

As we discussed in Chapter 1, child abuse did not receive public visibility until the identification of battered baby syndrome by Kempe in 1962, and it was only then that child abuse began to be reconfigured as a medical and not just a social concern. As Evans (2004) indicates, the adoption of the term 'syndrome' reflected this new approach to non-accidental injury (NAI), and the leading role that paediatricians were playing in 'fighting' this medical problem.

The identification of SBS (or 'whiplash shaken infant syndrome' as it was initially known) in the 1970s by John Caffey was a consequence of the redefinition of professional boundaries and the occupational identity of paediatrics. For instance, Halpern (1990) showed that the post-war trend in paediatrics was geared towards the greater acceptance of 'psychosocial' problems in childhood such as learning difficulties, developmental disability and child abuse, and not only focusing on strictly biomedical concerns. This trend has been perceived as a move towards the 'medicalisation' of health problems in childhood to incorporate issues such as child abuse and neglect, by re-conceptualising them as scientific areas of medicine which should be regarded as central to the clinical work of the paediatrician. Richmond (1975) quoted in Halpern (1990 p.34) states:

> Just as in previous years we faced the complex problems of preventing infectious diseases, nutritional disorders, and metabolic problems, today we are challenged to find analogous approaches to

prevention and management of such complicated problems as child abuse and neglect, failure to thrive, learning problems, as well as developmental disabilities. Our research methods are those of the epidemiologist, biostatistician, and the social scientist.

According to this view, psychosocial care was increasingly being viewed as a legitimate area of paediatric practice, where medically uninteresting 'behavioural deviance' was becoming redefined as an intellectually challenging problem. It is within this professional context that a greater interest in child abuse subsequently emerged as a legitimate area of clinical interest and scientific research. What had previously been viewed as mundane and uninteresting clinical practice, became redefined partly as means of securing professional jurisdiction over psychosocial care, as well as biomedical work, in paediatrics.

In the 1870s, however, the public record of child abuse remained remarkably quiet, which was attributed to the high infant mortality rate both in the USA and many parts of Europe. Consequently, the impact of child abuse was overshadowed by the large public health concern that this presented for clinicians. Evans (2004) states that: 'the conquering of the major communicable diseases causing infant mortality may have freed up paediatricians to spend more time on behaviour and development' (p.162). Also, with the launch of the clinical field of paediatrics in 1888 the prevention and detection of childhood diseases received a professional platform that led to a greater interest in behavioural and developmental problems (Brosco 2002).

Constructing shaken baby syndrome

In 1962 Kempe *et al.* identified the 'battered baby syndrome', recognising for the first time in modern times the possibility that young children were often the victims of physical abuse. Although NAI in children was recognised as far back as 1860 (Tardieu), the impetus for the recent growth in awareness in NAHI came from the USA with the publication of a landmark research study on the 'whiplash shaken infant syndrome' by John Caffey (1972), a paediatric radiologist. Caffey's research represented a milestone because it identified the clinical features of a specific form of child abuse, and its probable causal mechanism, that moved beyond the general speculation that previously surrounded NAI in children. It also represented the development of a new hypothesis for the manifestation of retinal and intracranial haemorrhages that would previously have been either un-diagnosed or treated as unknown or unexplained. Caffey's 'whiplash shaken infant syndrome' was used to describe a constellation of clinical findings in infants which included intracranial (within the skull) and intraocular (within the eyes) haemorrhages in the absence of signs of exter-nal trauma or skull fracture. For Caffey it became clear that in the absence of witnessed accidental trauma, the most probable cause had to be non-accidental, such as through 'shaking'. His hypothesis has subsequently been redefined as SBS, as it is more commonly recognised today.

Caffey's focus on the external rather than internal causal mechanisms has attracted criticism that the hypothesis necessarily neglects the possibil-ity of a congenital or pathological cause such as meningitis or certain viral infections. However, although Caffey did not dismiss the likelihood of an internal cause, on the basis of his research the most probable reason for most cases of bleeding within the retinas and the cranium was believed to be non-accidental. Since Caffey's research it has become widely recognised by paediatricians that in very young children the most probable cause of the clinical signs described above was likely to be external trauma, that usually involved 'shaking' the child. Subsequently, the shaken baby hypothesis was extended to include retinal and subdural haemorrhages and swelling of the brain, which were widely recognised as the signature marks of whiplash injuries caused through shaking. Other clinical signs associated with SBS have since been broadened even further to include rib fractures or bruising, fractures of the long bones and external head trauma, although there is con-troversy as to whether shaking necessarily includes some element of direct impact (Duhaime 1988).

In recent years, however, the basis of the shaken baby hypothesis has increasingly been the object of criticism largely due to the lack of objective scientific evidence to support the 'shaking' theory, or to disprove it, for that matter. To this end the challenge levelled at SBS does have a legitimate goal in seeking to find answers to a problem that is clouded in mystery even today. It is this challenge from within medicine itself that has more recently provided the impetus for the re-examination of the syndrome.

Deconstructing shaken baby syndrome

In Chapter 5 we examine in greater detail the medical controversy that has surrounded SBS in recent years. However, for the purposes of this chapter we will trace some of the current attempts in medicine to 'deconstruct' the shaken baby hypothesis, by drawing on debates from within the scientific community. We begin by summarising some of the criticisms of SBS, and why we view this as an attempt by an increasing number of clinicians and other scientists to 'deconstruct' the hypothesis. We view the 'backlash' against SBS as an attempt to move the parameters within which clinical pae-diatrics operates and seeks to define its professional boundaries. The conflict between those who want paediatrics to become more scientific and to move away from psychosocial matters and those who prefer to embrace psychosocial problems as a central component of paediatric practice began in the 1960s, and has recently resurfaced as the debate about the causes of childhood injury have become the subject of critical examination in certain high profile legal cases.

The clinical position

The first criticism levelled at SBS emphasises the lack of objective scientific evidence to support the theory. Probably the most uncertain aspect of the hypothesis is the debate over the degree of force that is required to bring about the injuries to the brain and retina that are commonly thought to occur as a result of shaking. Duhaime *et al.* (1987) conducted an experiment to determine the susceptibility of the infant brain to a shaking injury. They concluded that severe head injuries commonly diagnosed as shaking inju-ries required impact to occur and that shaking alone was unlikely to cause the injuries. Despite this research, uncertainty continues to persist about the need for the victim to sustain an impact against a solid surface for such inju-ries to appear. Moreover, if an impact is necessary to cause the injuries exhibited by children who have allegedly been shaken, it is still unclear how much force is required. Advocates of the shaken baby hypothesis have claimed that the force required to inflict subdural and retinal haemorrhages is equivalent to a fall from a two-storey building or a motor vehicle accident. However, none of these claims have been substantiated under scientific con-ditions, and the consequent research evidence remains limited. Those who object to the shaken baby hypothesis suggest that only falls of a short dis-tance are necessary to cause subdural haemorrhages. In a letter submitted to the American Journal of Forensic Medicine and Pathology in 1998, Plunkett claims:

> There is no experimental data on immature skulls or brains, and we
> do not know the amount of force required to cause a subdural, reti-
> nal haemorrhage and brain injury in a child. However, adult data

(human and other primates) and anecdotal evidence from children who have suffered clearly accidental head injuries from short distance falls indicate that an impact velocity [from a short fall] will cause a subdural. (Plunkett 1998)

This conclusion, which suggests that impact on its own, and from a short fall, can cause a subdural bleed stands directly opposed to the shaken baby hypothesis, whose advocates contend that shaking is also necessary to produce the injuries commonly seen in these cases. The general position adopted by critics of SBS has been to question the credibility of the shaken baby hypothesis by showing that the scientific evidence does not support its existence. By casting enough doubt on the proposition that shaking alone is sufficient to produce subdural and retinal haemorrhages, the critics hoped to question the very existence of the hypothesis. One way that they have attempted to achieve this goal, as illustrated above, was by suggesting that short fall impacts could lead to the same type of injuries that are commonly seen when a child is violently shaken. Plunkett (1998) contends that supporters of the shaken baby hypothesis have confusingly treated *clinical experience* as *science*, arguing that the sum of vast clinical experience may be knowledge but it is not science. However, this position assumes that injuries which are characteristic of shaking can be explained conclusively without reference to the more 'indeterminate' clinical experience of the clinician. We return to this issue again in Chapter 5.

The argument that retinal haemorrhages, in combination with subdural haemorrhages, are indicative of a shaking injury has been subject to similar criticism, especially as retinal haemorrhages can also result from other types of retinal pathology that are indistinguishable from those caused by shaking. For instance, vascular malformations or arachnoid cysts can also be found in association with retinal bleeding. Plunkett claims that SBS has evolved, and its advocates have adapted certain elements of the theory in response to growing criticism of the hypothesis, suggesting that it is nothing more than a theory which frequently fails to stand up to scientific examination:

I am reminded of Abraham's negotiations with God regarding Sodom and Gomorrah: 'Well, if not multilayered flame shaped haemorrhage, how about multilayered flame shaped haemorrhage with macular folds?' If the latest version of the 'pathognomic sign' proves to be correct, it is still no more than a marker for a rotational

> deceleration injury, and does not tell us if the cause of the injury was a 'shaken-slam' or a high-strain rotational fall. (Plunkett 1998)

As this statement suggests, advocates of SBS have adapted their views about the nature of retinal haemorrhages (RH) in order to explain challenges to the nature of the signs. However, as Plunkett has shown, this still does not explain whether the injury had been accidental or a result of abuse because the nature of the head injury is not specific to the pathogenesis of RH. A recent case history of a child who presented with a specific type of RH – 'perimacular retinal folds' – illustrates the danger of relying on certain 'diagnostic' hallmarks as indicators of child abuse, which may subsequently prove to be wrong.

A study was conducted by Lantz *et al.* (2004) on the causes of perimacular retinal folds where the retina buckles due to head trauma. The study was prompted by the death of a 14-month-old child who had the condition after a television crushed his head. However, child protection agencies removed a three-year-old sibling from the home because the retinal haemorrhages and retinal folds were thought to be diagnostic of NAHI. Although the three-year-old sibling corroborated the father's account, the paediatric ophthalmologist concluded that perimacular retinal folds were diagnostic of SBS. This example illustrates the danger of relying on scientific hypotheses without fully considering the wider context within which such injuries occur. Lantz *et al.* (2004) proclaim:

> Statements in the medical literature that perimacular retinal folds are diagnostic of shaken baby syndrome are not supported by objective scientific evidence. Non-comparative observational reports and unsystematic narrative review articles contain insufficient evidence to provide unbiased support for or against diagnostic specificity, and inferences about associations, causal or otherwise, cannot be determined… Until good evidence is available, we urge caution in interpreting eye findings out of context. (p.756)

The argument proposed here states that perimacular retinal folds cannot be assumed to result from non-accidental trauma, as distinct from accidental injury, as they are not specific only to SBS. Indeed, according to Lantz *et al.* it is difficult to distinguish between accidental and non-accidental injuries based on the clinical findings alone. In their review of the literature Lantz *et al.* found that none of the 42 studies that were identified had documented an accidental cause as a possibility for the retinal folds. Consequently, they report that the language used to describe perimacular retinal folds changed in the early 1990s as being *observed* in cases of SBS, to being *diagnostic* of SBS by the late 1990s. This was a leap of judgement which Lantz *et al.* believed was not supported by the research evidence, especially as accidental injuries are thought to bring about similar pathological changes in the retina. Consequently, the argument proposed here by Lantz *et al.* does not dispute an 'external' causal mechanism for perimacular retinal folds, but suggests that the greatest difficulty is in distinguishing between accident and abuse. Thus, they are suggesting that science alone cannot offer the answer to this problem and by implication the answer could reside in a thorough examination of the social context in which an injury has occurred.

The other problem that critics of the shaken baby hypothesis have attempted to address is related to whether the shearing of the membranes that surround the brain, or diffuse axonal injury (DAI), is responsible for causing death and brain damage. Plunkett (1998) contends that no scientific evidence exists to show that the shearing of blood vessels causes injury or death. The other criticism directed at proponents of SBS is their contention that DAI causes prolonged unconsciousness in victims. The conclusion is based on findings from studies conducted on adult brains and therefore, it is claimed, cannot be extrapolated to similar injuries in infants. This evidence has subsequently been used to conclude that infants who are shaken do not experience a 'lucid' interval, as this was not apparent in adults, and that all deaths are caused by axonal injury. In response, the critics argue that the evidence simply does not exist to support this view, and the cause of death could be due to a range of reasons, as Plunkett illustrates: 'We simply do not know why some of these children die: it might be axonal injury, malignant cerebral edema, direct irritation of brain-stem breathing centres, or some other phenomenon we have not considered' (1998). Moreover, Plunkett suggests that the tendency among advocates of SBS to use over simplified statements such as 'immediately unconscious' or 'globally changed' to draw a direct link with the possibility of physical abuse, are also not supported by the scientific evidence. Such statements, he suggests, lead to unsubstantiated claims and assumptions, often implying that 'The last person standing when the music stopped is the one who must have injured the child' (1998).

There is currently a desire among a number of health professionals to abandon the term SBS as it presupposes child abuse, and therefore negates the possibility of accidental trauma or other underlying pathological or neurological cause. In a similar vein, judges have also indicated a preference for the more neutral term NAHI (*R v Harris and others* (2005), para 56). Those who have opposed the shaken baby hypothesis have stated the need for paediatricians to recognise that RH are at best an external marker for a *possible* head injury, which should not automatically be viewed as non-accidental. They claim that it is also important to acknowledge that the evidence for a lucid interval in a child following a rotational head injury and DAI may not explain why some children die quickly and others experience a symptom-free interval prior to death. Plunkett (1998) argues that we need to differentiate between what we scientifically know to be true and what we think or hope to be true. He argues that modern medicine offers many examples of medical technologies and treatments that were believed to be effective, only subsequently to be demonstrated to be ineffective or untrue and provides examples that illustrate this misconception, such as the routine use of foetal monitors and routine skull X-rays in children with head injuries, both of which were subsequently shown to be unreliable in detecting clinical abnormalities.

Although we address the other side of the argument posited by those who support the shaken baby hypothesis in Chapter 5, the critique provided above serves to show why the assumptions often made by child abuse professionals have not escaped scientific and, as we shall later show, public scrutiny. The scientific questions that have been raised in relation to the uncertainties surrounding the shaken baby hypothesis are still a long way from being resolved, despite recent research that has cast doubt on some of the issues raised above.

The 'medicalisation' thesis

Can the recent controversy over the scientific basis of SBS be viewed as an attempt by medical professionals to redefine an essentially 'social' phenomenon in terms of a medical problem? In sociology, broadly speaking, two types of debate have ensued in relation to the question of medicalisation of behavioural, psychological and social problems: first, the *extent* to which these have been medicalised or subject to medical control – questions of degree, and, second, the *nature* of the medical practices that have led to their medicalisation – questions of *process*. In this section we focus on the latter forms of medical control or questions relating to the way that behavioural problems, and physical child abuse more specifically, have been treated as medical problems. We first provide a definition of medicalisation and describe the nature of medical control of social and behavioural 'deviance' before embarking upon an analysis of the means through which medicine has sought to classify child abuse using a medical, rather than a social, conceptualisation.

We adopt Peter Conrad's (1979) definition of medicalisation, framed from the perspective of the medical control of 'deviance'. We use this definition predominantly because our main concern in this book is a form of behavioural deviance, the infliction of NAHI in children, which by the nature of the subject presupposes an abnormal or deviant origin or cause. The point of departure for the book is the examination of 'non-accidental' and therefore abusive head injury in young children, which consequently implies that the origin of the injury must be a social, not a medical one. We believe that this is a reasonable position to adopt because nobody doubts that child abuse occurs, and therefore it has to have a social definition. However, this is not to deny that accidents are also a major cause of head injury and that the manifestation of certain clinical features can have a pathological origin. Nevertheless, just as people's personal experiences of illness are shaped socially, they also have to be distinct from medical definitions. For instance, the individual may experience an illness episode in terms of headaches or chest discomfort, whereas a medical professional may rationalise the illness experience as a benign viral infection. The patient, however, may experience the illness in a more negative way, through constantly feeling sick and being unable to resume normal functioning, whereas the doctor may understand the illness episode as a common infection that will soon pass. These two perspectives illustrate the difference between the medical view which locates the illness within the biomedical paradigm and redefines it as 'disease', and the patient's perception which encompasses his or her wider physical as well as social experience of suffering from the illness. Thus, at the centre of the medicalisation thesis is the contention that anything that can remotely be viewed as illness should have a medical basis. Part and parcel of the medicalisation process are its controlling consequences over behavioural practices and behaviours (wittingly or unwittingly).

According to Conrad (1979), medicine functions to secure adherence to social norms, specifically by using medical means to minimise or remove deviant behaviour. Thus, patients with schizophrenia are prescribed antipsychotic drugs in order to relieve their symptoms, to help them resume 'normal' functioning and to prevent them from behaving 'abnormally'. In relation to SBS, the medicalisation argument is more complex because recently we have reached a stage where there is no medical consensus for the existence of the hypothesis or the causal mechanism for SDH and RH. Nonetheless, the priority for those medical professionals opposed to the shaken baby hypothesis is not to establish medical control through educating 'at risk' groups of the most effective prevention strategies (public health strategies) but by redefining an essentially social phenomenon as a medical problem with a clinical aetiology (cause). The arguments posited by critics of SBS, illustrated in the previous section, are examples of the desire to identify a clinical origin for the signs often associated with SBS. At the same time, these arguments also strongly negate or attempt to diminish the credibility of the 'social' explanation, which suggests that SDH and RH are often associated with non-accidental trauma in young children.

We now turn our attention to three types of medical control identified by Conrad (1979) with which we will examine the medicalisation of SBS: science and medical technology, medical collaboration and medical ideology.

Science and medical technology

Medical social control is related to the acceptance of a medical perspective as the dominant definition of a certain issue, problem, or phenomenon. As medical definitions become accepted into mainstream life, they subsequently suppress competing definitions, often because medicine adopts science or scientific explanations to legitimate its position. One pertinent example is the medical control of pregnancy. Barker (1998) has shown that during the twentieth century, pre-natal care had been appropriated by medicine and institutionalised into the hospital setting. It is argued that pregnancy had been cast as 'disease-like' and the woman had come to be defined around her identity as patient. Likewise, biomedicine dismissed folk wisdom, especially when used by pregnant women for symptom relief such as morning sickness, by defining it as backward and ultimately dangerous. Experiential knowledge of the expectant mother was replaced by the physician's expertise and (usually) *his* medical knowledge. Technology had also helped to harness the medicalisation of childbirth, where the rationale was that pregnancy was potentially complex and could lead to complications, and therefore required medical technologies such as foetal monitors to reduce the risk of complications. Elevated blood pressure, whilst undetectable by the woman, now required medical surveillance such as with the use of blood pressure monitors. Conrad and Schneider (1992) suggest that medicalisation is the direct consequence of the expansion of rationalism and science. Barker supports this:

> Facts about the physical body generated through this paradigm create what is assumed to be a universal (normal) composite of the body from which deviations are recognised as abnormal. This normal-abnormal binary legitimates diagnoses, treatments and/or medically prescribed behavioural changes. (1998, p.1072)

As this illustrates, there is a shift from self care to medical supervision, as well as a shift from preventative strategies to medical treatments, and an emphasis on monitoring pregnancies using technology. So how does this argument about medical control relate to the case of SBS?

The case of SBS is similar to the pregnancy example outlined above as both have witnessed attempts by medicine to re-conceptualise a phenomenon as 'medical', which hitherto has been viewed as a 'social' process. However, the mechanics of medical control are qualitatively different in the case of SBS. First, a medical consensus exists in relation to pregnancy about the need for medical intervention and medical surveillance to minimise complications. In SBS a consensus has not yet been reached about the appropriateness of relying on a medical interpretation of the syndrome, without acknowledging the possible 'external' and social influences on the issue of causality. In other words, health professionals are in the midst of a debate about the likely causes of SBS, and whether the hypothesis should be viewed in purely medical terms. Plunkett (1998), for instance, suggests that we need to abandon the term 'shaken-slammed infant syndrome' and use an actual description of the injury mechanism, such as 'rotational deceleration'. In a similar way the term 'pregnancy' was changed to 'antenatal' care, which encompassed a broader definition of care for the expectant mother, whereas pregnancy was more culturally specific and limited primarily to foetal care. Thus, antenatal was a more objective and culturally neutral term which encompassed the medical care of the woman's health, and not only the health of the foetus, prior to birth.

Second, those who oppose the shaken baby hypothesis have sought to provide an alternative medical definition by drawing upon science to legitimise their view. We will explore this argument in much more detail in Chapter 5, but in brief critics of SBS have tried to explain SBS with reference to the hypothesis that 'oxygen starvation' to the brain (hypoxia) could account for the SDH and RH in infants, challenging the belief that the cause was necessarily external, as would be expected if a child had been shaken (Geddes *et al.* 2001). This recent research has been widely used by opponents of SBS, in subsequent legal cases, the media and in academic publications to strengthen the case for a medical (pathological) explanation for the shaken baby hypothesis. The aim was to redefine SBS as a biomedical rather than a social phenomenon.

Previously, with the creation of the shaken baby hypothesis, medicine was able to secure control over its definition, and with the work of Caffey (1972) the syndrome had become widely accepted by the medical establishment. Just as changes within medicine enabled doctors to recognise and treat behavioural disorders and medical trauma, technological advances facilitated the ability of clinicians to identify pathologies and signs of trauma that previously could not be clinically detected. Indeed, X-rays and magnetic resonance imaging (MRI) scans provided unbiased evidence that was previously unavailable, since doctors could only rely on histories provided by carers, which were frequently subject to high levels of bias. Paediatricians were able to confirm NAI through employing x-rays to detect fractures, and MRI scans of the baby's head to detect subdural haemorrhages and brain swelling. Therefore, through the use of advanced medical technologies, the medical profession was able to establish further medical control over the diagnosis and treatment of accidental as well as non-accidental injuries, where attempts could be made at distinguishing the two through the use of medical technology. As Evans contends, the placement of child abuse into the hospital setting, where such technology was freely accessible for the child health practitioner, facilitated the detailed study and identification of complex forms of child abuse such as SBS:

> Hospital based practices provided these academic physicians with the critical mass of abused children to note patterns of injuries and their institutional affiliation gave academic physicians the freedom to make socially and legally charged diagnoses that could have been professionally risky for private practitioners. (2004, p.162)

As medicine had come to accept the existence of child abuse, the debate had moved from whether medicine had a legitimate role in the recognition and detection of NAI, to the question of *how* such cases should be interpreted: either as a social phenomenon or redefined as a medical problem. Both camps, the opponents and advocates of the shaken baby hypothesis, have sought to strengthen their cause and ultimately their control over the definition of the syndrome through collaboration with other authorities involved in child protection.

Medical collaboration

Medicine not only acts as an independent agent of social control but collaboration with other authorities often helps to strengthen its social control functions. Conrad suggests that such collaboration involves acting as 'information provider, gatekeeper, institutional agent, and technician' (1979, p.5) emphasising the interwoven nature of medicine in the fabric of society. Medical collaboration in cases of child abuse most frequently occurs in relation to the 'information provider' and 'gatekeeper' role that is adopted by the medical professional. First, the clinician is sanctioned by the nature of his or her role to report suspected cases of child abuse to child protection agencies. At this stage the collaborative nature of the clinical role is apparent when the clinician is usually expected to provide an expert opinion on the probable cause of the injury, often to a child protection conference. These conferences are multidisciplinary events, often attended by professional representatives from social work, psychiatry, police, nursing and medicine, and it is here that decisions often hinge on the medical advice of the clinician. The doctor's opinion is primarily responsible for determining the severity and nature of the injuries, as well as the likelihood that they could be non-accidental. Consequently, medical influence over the direction that the initial investigation takes is paramount, and this control is further strengthened because of the requirement in civil cases to show that on balance of probability the child had been abused.

As we discuss in Chapter 4, the threshold of proof is lower in civil proceedings than in criminal proceedings and hence the room for doubt in medical judgement so much greater in deciding whether abuse has taken place. Thus, even if doctors have a degree of doubt about the causes of the injuries, this rule allows them to apply judgement relatively flexibly without the risk of sanction and confers on them a high level of control over the decision-making process. In summary, the medical professional's information provider and gatekeeper role in the initial reporting of suspected cases of abuse, and in subsequent case conferences, enables them to exercise substantial influence in defining the cause and nature of the suspected injuries incurred by young children. In our research cohort, we found that medical opinion was central to the outcome of case conferences, and conflicting medical opinion usually led to a decision by the Crown Prosecution Service not to initiate criminal proceedings. On the other hand, a consensus in medical opinion that the injuries were indicative of abuse often resulted in a criminal trial and in a care order application by the social services. It can be concluded that medical advice during the initial investigation is central to the outcome in such cases.

The examples of medical collaboration provided above show how medicine performs reporting, definitional and technical tasks for other institutions, in our example the child protection and criminal justice agencies. However, according to Conrad (1979), medicine is also constrained by its relationship with other institutions. In legal proceedings, as in cases of SBS, medical expertise or judgement is often scrutinised and criticised by the demands of the collaborating institution (the court of law) or by the competing arguments of other professionals or clinicians who hold a different opinion. Consequently, medical social control is rarely left unchecked and does not exhibit unlimited freedom to impose its definition on a particular issue or problem. In child abuse cases medical definitions and concepts are most effectively challenged not by the collaborating institution, but by those within the medical profession itself. Thus, the question of causality (whether the cause is accidental or non-accidental) in SBS is most strongly disputed by clinicians themselves, and the issue of definition is limited to a choice between two alternative medical explanations: accident or abuse. Medical control over the definition and explanation of SBS is not in question, but what is in dispute is whether the syndrome should be left as it is or redefined as a medical phenomenon. The suggestion by Plunkett (1998) above to discard the term SBS and replace it with an objectively 'neutral' label such as 'rotational deceleration' force is a prime example of the challenge to the mechanism of injury.

Indeed, it is claimed by opponents of SBS that doctors who support the shaken baby hypothesis have somehow been influenced by their emotions in their association with non-clinicians such as social workers, police and charities, all with a vested interest in demonstrating the widespread existence of NAI in young children. In fact, Plunkett (1998) refers to paediatricians, paediatric neurologists, radiologists and pathologists who advocate the existence of SBS and other types of child abuse as the 'child abuse professionals'. This appears to be a derogatory term that seeks to demean and discredit the validity of their clinical knowledge, by suggesting that their area of expertise is not science but 'child abuse'. In summary, medical collaboration might include non-medical institutions as well as clinical medicine, and the process not only promotes medical control but frequently curtails it. Medical collaborations with non-medical institutions can help to strengthen medicine's hold over 'social' experiences and behavioural problems, but they can also restrict its control through external (or internal) examination of the scientific evidence.

Medical ideology

The third type of medical social control is what Conrad (1979, p. 6) refers to as 'medical ideology'. Accordingly, he states that: '*Medical ideology* is a type of social control that involves defining a behaviour or condition as an illness primarily because of the social and ideological benefits accrued by conceptualizing it in medical terms.' According to Conrad the latent functions of medical ideology serve the interests of individual members, professions or the dominant interests of society, but they do not have an organic basis in disease. One classic example of the way the dominant interests of society have been reinforced by medicine's social control of human behaviour is evident in the case of urban violence. In 1970 a neurosurgeon and a psychiatrist published a book in which it was claimed that urban violence, often referring to African Americans as an example, was not caused by social oppression and deprivation but by 'brain dysfunction' for which they recommended psychosurgery (Mark and Ervin 1970). Similarly, in 1851 Dr Samuel Cartwright, a leading authority on the medical care of African Americans at the time, identified 'drapetomia' which was coined the disease of African American slaves (Cartwright 1851). The main symptom of this medical condition was to abscond or run away from the captors. Cartwright believed that the 'disease' was perfectly curable using preventative strategies such as 'whipping'. He suggested treating slaves like children who needed to be kept in a submissive state.

The passing of time does not appear to have diminished the attraction of explaining human behaviour using the medical paradigm. Since the mapping of the human genome, there has been a dramatic increase in the types of condition, medical as well as behavioural, that are thought to have a genetic basis. Recently, scientists have attributed obsessive-compulsive disorder, criminal behaviour, drug and alcohol addiction, aggression and even predisposition to religious beliefs to their genotype. It is thought that the temporal lobes, which control hearing, speech and memory, might predispose some people to religious beliefs and hallucinations. Apparently, the intensity of religious beliefs is not considered as a function of people's social conditioning and their experience of significant life events. Is it possible that medicine is making a similar simplistic assumption in its desire to define SBS as a medical condition?

The ideological relevance of attempts at redefining SBS as a medical pathology rather than a social phenomenon is an apparently moral one, because, as the argument goes, innocent people are being mistakenly prosecuted on the basis of scientific inconsistencies and flawed evidence. The opportunity for critics of SBS to argue their case successfully has never been better, as the desire of the legal system to protect innocent people from wrongful prosecution appears to be greater than the need to protect the victims. The emphasis on avoiding wrongful convictions in court is also high on the agenda within the high echelons of the medical profession, as exemplified by the desire of the General Medical Council to maintain public confidence in the ability of medical professionals to act responsibly when providing an expert opinion in court. The attempt to remove Professor Sir Roy Meadow from the medical register, which we discuss in Chapter 6, is an example of the need to secure the trust of the public.

The reluctant imperialism of medicine

So far in this chapter, we have explored the historical emergence of the shaken baby hypothesis, the subsequent challenges that have been directed at it largely from within medicine, and the prevailing medical control or medicalisation of child abuse. We have also shown how medicine has treated SBS as a form of social deviance requiring a thorough 'medical' and therefore scientific interpretation of the phenomenon. Moreover, to date medicine has been responsible for providing the scientific explanations for many forms of childhood injuries, both to child protection agencies as well as to courts. However, at the turn of the twenty-first century a slightly different picture is beginning to emerge, whereby the public and the legal system have raised concerns about the credibility and accuracy of medical evidence. In this final section we provide a brief examination of how far some of the recent challenges to medical dominance, especially in legal cases of SBS, have succeeded in undermining medical control and dominance in this area of child protection. In the first instance, however, we illustrate an important issue that seems to challenge the medicalisation thesis, at least in part, illustrating the reluctance of medicine to usurp control over non-medical problems.

De Swaan (1989) claims that medicine occupies a strategic place in society, where the potential for medical intervention is widening, and medical expertise is invoked in situations that are beyond the competence and knowledge-base of doctors. According to the author, the main reason for this expanding encroachment of medicine into areas that traditionally have not been perceived as a clinical terrain is the resolution of social conflict. However, De Swaan argues that medicine has in actual fact always been reluctant to expand its authority when given the opportunity mainly because it is at this level that difficulties of maintaining professional consensus frequently arise. The power base of the profession rests on the unanimity of the scientific community (in public view at least). Institutions involved in social conflict, as demonstrated in the recent cases of SBS in the courts, usually seek a medical solution to their predicament. However, what these conflicts usually lead to, especially when the scientific basis of medical knowledge is insufficient for the resolution of these conflicts, is the threat of open controversy within the profession itself. Such action could undermine professional unanimity in scientific areas of inquiry, which is a central source of power and authority of the medical profession. In support of this proposition De Swaan states:

> Medical authority is invoked ever more frequently, also in situations that are outside the scope of scientific justification. The main but latent function of this medicalization is the resolution of social conflict. This occurs more often than not in tacit collusion between a work organisation (or the wider community) on the one hand, the individualized 'patient' on the other hand and the doctor as the arbiter who defines socially contested issues in terms of medical problems. As scientific medicine provides insufficient justification of these medical interventions, they threaten to become the subject of open controversy within the organized medical profession and thus to undermine professional unanimity, and with it the authority of the profession as a whole. (p.1165)

It perhaps does not appear at first hand that medicine is a reluctant participant in the identification and the development of expertise in the area of child abuse, as medical experts have often provided evidence in court on a voluntary basis. Waitzkin (1983) has advanced the 'medical imperialism' thesis which suggests that medicine is expansionist in nature, just like many other organisations in contemporary capitalist society, seeking to further their interests. However, De Swaan (1989) contends that the threat of open conflict and controversy has led medicine to exercise caution and restraint in expanding into other areas of practice. Despite this view medicine has expanded its boundaries, not of its own choosing but because its services were often required (and still are) by other institutions and organisations, such as the legal system's demand for medical expert evidence in complex child abuse cases. De Swaan states that the reason why medicine expanded despite its hesitation 'was in part the unintended and combined result of myriads of interventions by individual doctors, in social conflicts, in tacit collusion with the parties involved' (1989, p.1168).

Moreover, the extension of medical influence beyond the confines of its scientific legitimacy also exposed its competence to public scrutiny and political or legal debate 'precisely on those issues where the profession was vulnerable by definition, as its policies could not be fully justified on the grounds of medical expertise, the only base of legitimacy for its exercise of power' (p.1168). An example of such open public scrutiny is evident in the Court of Appeal's decision in *R v Harris and others* (2005) to quash the convictions of two alleged shaken baby cases and reduce one to manslaughter, which we discuss in detail in Chapter 6. This example serves to show how medical authority can be openly undermined when it seeks to assert its control over areas of expertise that are not strictly medical, or where its scientific base is limited. As De Swaan (1989) contends, institutions or agencies involved in conflict, as in the example provided above, often seek a medical solution. However, the reason that 'external' agencies can undermine medicine's ability to define social problems through the adoption of a medical discourse is because those very agencies also possess a certain degree of 'proto-professionalism', a medical knowledge base with which this task can be achieved. For instance, De Swaan states: 'The successful reformulation of their dispute in technical scientific terms already presupposes a certain measure of familiarity on their part with the basic notions and fundamental stances of the medical profession' (1989, p.1167). Illustrative of this is the ability of legal practitioners to gain a sufficient understanding of the medical and social issues, which equips them with the knowledge to engage proactively in medical debate in legal proceedings. As the Attorney General commented in his review of 88 cases of NAHI in young children, which was initiated after the case of Angela Canning and which we examine in detail in Chapter 6:

> The evidence given was carefully examined by the Court of Appeal
> [in *R v Harris and others* (2005)] over a number of days. It was in a

very good position, therefore, to reach conclusions on some of the hotly disputed medical issues that have been found in the medical literature on the issue. (Attorney General 2006, para 9)

However, of even greater interest is the apparent ability of the legal system to appear to 'resolve' the controversy, at least from the vantage point of the law. We continue with this theme in the final section.

Keeping public confidence: law and medicine working together?

In view of what has been discussed above, it is not surprising that medicine has been somewhat reluctant to engage in legal battles to prove or disprove this or that condition, syndrome or disease. The cost of exposure to an adversarial legal system is often high for individual experts, who, prior to the ruling of the High Court in *Meadow v General Medical Council* (2006), risked disciplinary action by the General Medical Council, even in circumstances where the provision of expert evidence had been in 'good faith'. As we discuss in Chapter 6, the recent 'bad' press that medical experts have received has not helped the long-term cause of the judiciary to encourage the 'reluctant' medical expert witness to engage willingly in legal proceedings in cases that are not traditionally the domain of medicine, such as child abuse. However, the High Court in ruling *Meadow* sends a most welcome message to expert witnesses providing evidence to the courts in future, as the implication of the ruling is that individual doctors will not be subject to disciplinary proceedings for unintended mistakes (which are more likely to occur in complex cases) and that the process by which evidence is appraised and evaluated needs to take greater responsibility.

Furthermore, by 2006, the judgement of the Court of Appeal in *R v Harris and others* (2005) and the outcome of the Attorney General's review of cases of SBS (Attorney General 2006), both of which we examine in detail in Chapter 6, seem to indicate that the pendulum is beginning to swing in the opposite direction, largely in support of the shaken baby hypothesis. The combined effect of these two factors has arguably been to help strengthen public confidence in, and to encourage medical experts to engage with, the legal process.

CHAPTER 3

Clinical Identification of Non-Accidental Head Injury: Examining the 'Social' Risk Factors

In this chapter we address two fundamental concerns facing health professionals in the identification of traumatic non-accidental injury (NAI) in young children. First, we address the question: what are the social risk factors of NAI and how might these be identified? In so doing we explore the core issues reported in the literature in relation to the problems encountered by health professionals in detecting NAI. Second, we discuss our own research findings on non-accidental head injury (NAHI) in infants, to highlight the main social issues, problems and consequences of identifying NAI in young children. We end the chapter with an analysis of the shortfalls in current practices of identifying abused children and those at risk of abuse and propose potential solutions, based on professional, inter-agency and organisational restructuring of child protection systems.

Identification and reporting of non-accidental injury

The level of reporting of child physical abuse to child protection agencies is lower than would be expected from local prevalence statistics, indicating that many victims of abuse are not being identified (Sidebotham and Pearce 1997). One of a number of possible reasons for this discrepancy is the 'culture of disbelief' that child abuse does not actually exist. The other reason is the uncertainty about what child abuse is and how it is defined. The definition of child abuse continues to be an area of contention in child protection especially when the evidence is not clear and when practitioners do not know how to interpret the evidence, whether it is clinical or social. Media coverage of child deaths and cases of serious child abuse has drawn attention to the contested nature of scientific evidence, possibly fuelling scepticism about the very nature and existence of certain kinds of non-accidental harm. In recent years, however, medical practitioners have been made more aware of NAI in childhood, and have started to acknowledge the importance of identifying it on presentation to hospital (Kempe *et al.* 1962). Despite this, the research evidence suggests that many cases still remain undetected (Haeringen, Dadds and Armstrong 1998; Jenny *et al.* 1999; Sundell 1997). In this first section of the chapter we examine the problems facing health professionals, predominantly within the clinical setting, in the course of identifying and reporting possible cases of NAI in young children, and offer an analysis of how detection might be made more effective.

The literature on the identification of NAI in children is extensive and there is a significant overlap between the identification of child abuse by health professionals working within the clinical setting and by professionals from other agencies such as the police and social services. Typically, clinical professionals raise suspicion of abuse mainly because they are the first point of contact for those who have sustained such injuries, although the training among clinicians is highly inconsistent and awareness of possible NAI may well be limited among nurses and doctors. In this chapter we concentrate on the problems and barriers facing clinical staff in this difficult task. We revisit some of the difficulties incumbent in multi-agency communication in the subsequent section when we take a closer look at the findings from our own research on NAHI in young children. We have limited our analysis to the identification of NAI in clinical settings because the evidence strongly indicates that accident and emergency departments (A&E) are failing to identify children at risk of abuse as well as those who have been abused (Jenny *et al.* 1999; Sidebotham and Pearce 1997). Health professionals have a significant responsibility in identifying NAI and their actions often have far reaching consequences for the victims and their carers.

Clinical decisions to report suspected cases of NAI are not well documented, and much of the evidence is based on self-administered surveys by clinicians who might be inclined to report 'organisational' barriers to reporting, such as a lack of time, or reluctance to participate in child protection proceedings. This might involve attending multi-agency child protection conferences, writing medical reports and acting as expert witnesses in legal proceedings. The additional time and effort required to participate in the child protection process might be viewed as a disincentive for many clinicians. Studies have also tended to pay limited attention to the role of subjective clinical assessments, identifying the interpersonal factors that influence medical decisions in raising suspicion of NAI, such as the socio-economic status, age or racial background of the carers. Consequently, the scope of the research evidence for referral and non-referral to child protection agencies is somewhat limited. However, the evidence that does exist seems to suggest that the clinical identification of suspected NAI might sometimes be based on the clinician's subjective opinion rather than on a thorough examination of the clinical findings. One study, for instance, found that infants who were severely symptomatic as a result of head trauma were more likely to be referred to child protection agencies than infants with less severe symptoms (Jenny *et al.* 1999). This finding is supported by other studies, which raises the question of how often abused children are not detected, or investigated, because they present with visibly mild symptoms (Morris, Johnson and Clasen 1985; Sanders *et al.* 2003). Moreover, this proposition also indicates that the weight attached to different levels of injury, and subsequent referral patterns, are influenced by a clinician's subjective assessment of each case and not only by the clinical signs.

Clinicians, of course, also differ in their willingness to accept explanations that imply a non-accidental cause for *serious* head injury. Some studies have shown that the likelihood of reporting a suspected case of child abuse is dependent on the expertise of the treating clinician and their awareness of the 'tell-tale' signs of NAI (Haeringen *et al.* 1998). Medical practitioners in primary care, namely health visitors and general practitioners (GPs), are ideally placed to detect the clinical signs of possible NAI in very young children, especially in cases where they present with coexisting physical signs of neglect or abuse. However, there needs to be a greater concerted effort to educate GPs and health visitors, as well as other professionals in the community, to raise awareness of the pattern of injuries that are indicative of NAI. In recent years the responsibility for clinical child protection has largely passed to the community paediatrician, which has the advantage of utilising the skills of trained practitioners who can provide expert assessment and management based on extensive experience in community paediatrics (Royal College of Paediatricians and Child Health 2004). However, this tendency to rely on specialists means that the general or acute paediatrician may become deskilled in the recognition of physical child abuse. As most young children who are victims of severe child abuse will be admitted to hospital, this may have serious consequences for child protection and result in the under-recognition of abuse.

Is 'serious' non-accidental injury under-reported?

As we discussed in Chapter 1, very young children have been found to be particularly vulnerable to NAHI, with survivors often incurring serious long-term injuries. A study by Jayawant *et al.* (1998) conducted on 33 children under the age of two years with a subdural haemorrhage (SDH) revealed a strong association between a SDH and other types of non-accidental injury as well as a previous history of abuse in the family. They concluded that 82 per cent of the cases were due to child abuse, and only one case was due to a road traffic accident. However, no child protection referrals were subsequently made. The evidence suggests that in a significant proportion of young children, appropriate clinical investigations were not being conducted when a SDH was diagnosed. This finding is supported by our research. We also found that out of 68 cases presenting to hospital with a SDH, 14 had not been referred, and from these 14 cases 5 were suggestive of NAI on retrospective examination of the medical and social services records. We discuss this in more detail below. The research evidence, therefore, strongly suggests that most children under the age of 12 months who are admitted with a SDH to hospital have sustained these injuries as a result of physical abuse, with a smaller proportion of cases attributed to other causes such as a serious car accident or meningitis.

The research that has been conducted to date on the identification of NAI in young children shows that the procedures in place are limited and many cases of abuse remain undetected. Sidebotham and Pearce (1997) found that only 5.3 per cent of all children attending an A&E department in Bath, who were considered at risk of abuse according to standard risk assessment procedures, were referred to child protection professionals for further discussion of the risk to the child of future harm. Following an educational intervention, this figure increased to 13 per cent, which is still low, considering that these children were already identified as being at a 'high' risk of abuse. This research shows worrying signs that 87 per cent of children thought to be at high risk of abuse were not being identified following an educational intervention. Benger and McCabe (2001) report similar findings in relation to the presentation of children to A&E with burns and scalds, where referral rates of children who were thought to be at a high risk of abuse were poor, as was the general awareness of staff regarding the possibility of NAI. From this, it seems that clinical personnel in hospital departments do not engage in discussions about suspected high-risk cases of abuse, and commonly demonstrate a persistent lack of knowledge about the clinical and social risk factors. In addition, clinical staff rarely consulted the child protection register because it was too difficult and time consuming to gain access. Bureaucratic and inter-professional barriers to accessing confidential information about children from social services registers also led to long delays in the ability of clinicians to obtain a rapid assessment of each suspected case of abuse. These and other studies indicate that there is a culture of under-reporting of suspected NAI in children in A&E departments, which is largely to do with the fact that a significant proportion of medical and nursing staff receive no formal training in identifying potential indicators of child abuse and because they have no rapid access to a paediatric opinion (King and Reid 2003).

The clinical signs

Children can sustain a multitude of different categories of injuries, including minor injuries as well as multiple traumas, but it would be impractical, time consuming and unethical to conduct routine screening of every child presenting with physical injuries to A&E. However, research shows that the detection of NAI in children can be improved. It has been reported that all young children have restricted mobility, and injuries such as severe bruising, bone fractures or internal bleeding, which cannot be clinically explained, should suggest a strong suspicion of non-accidental injury (Merton and Carpenter 1990). As with fractures, the site of the bruising is highly significant because a young child is unlikely to sustain bruises accidentally on certain parts of the body, such as the face, abdomen, buttocks and ears (Atwal et al. 1998).

Barber and Sibert (2000) suggest that it is very rare for children over the age of three years to present with non-accidental bruising or fractures, in contrast to accidental causes. Indeed, non-accidental fractures were found to be most frequent in infants under the age of six months (Warlock, Stower and Barber 1986). The nature of bone injuries can also be a strong indicator of abuse. For instance, 'spiral' fractures, which cause the bone to bend and twist, are believed to be highly suggestive of abuse in very young children, and a study by Kemp, Mott and Sibert (1994) on non-accidental drowning found that there were no cases of non-accidental bath drowning over the age of 18 months, and all cases under this age drowned due to abuse or epilepsy. The emerging profile for these common injuries indicates that 'serious' or traumatic physical child abuse tends to occur in younger children. In the absence of a clinical or plausible accidental explanation, it could be concluded that these types of injuries are highly suggestive of abuse (Mathew, Ramamohan and Bennet 1998).

Bone fractures may not manifest outward signs and can be easily missed by the treating physician, especially in A&E where clinicians may not have the same expertise in identifying signs of abuse as in paediatrics. Therefore, some authors have recommended that children who present to A&E with associated injuries or signs that might suggest bone damage should receive a full skeletal survey (Barber and Sibert 2000). Barber and Sibert also recommend that a follow-up skeletal survey should be performed two weeks following first presentation to hospital for more accurate dating, and so that future episodes of abuse involving bone fractures are detected. Although clinical investigations can offer a profile of the likely pattern of injuries and offer clues as to whether they indicate a possible non-accidental cause, they cannot conclusively show on their own if the injuries were non-accidental. Consequently, the collection of social, personal and circumstantial evidence will usually be required to assist child protection professionals in determining the probable causes of the injuries.

Social risk factors of abuse

Having discussed the clinical indicators of NAI in young children, we now examine the social factors that have too frequently been overlooked by medical professionals in raising suspicion of NAI. Very limited primary and secondary research has been conducted on the problems that clinicians face when identifying NAI in children (Barber and Sibert 2000). However, studies have found that coexisting signs of abuse are a common feature among young children who present to hospital with injuries, suggesting that serious physical trauma are rarely isolated events (Sanders *et al.* 2003). Children with serious head injuries often present with other physical signs, which could add support to a suspicion of NAI. A further risk factor of abuse is the prior notification of physical injuries to a hospital or a GP (Andronicus *et al.* 1998).

However, unless the communication channels between clinical staff and other agencies such as social work and police are well established, information about any previous child protection concerns in relation to the victim will not be disclosed to front-line medical professionals. One possibility would be to develop a system of data sharing, so that A&E staff can have direct access to information regarding previous hospital admissions of a child, and where the information is linked to social services records of previous child protection concerns. The new responsibilities and working practices taking place following the recommendations of Lord Laming (Laming 2003) and the enactment of the Children Act 2004, and in particular the development of the Information Sharing Index which we discussed in Chapter 1, provide an ideal opportunity for enhanced data sharing between agencies. Once the Index is functional, clinical staff should be able to gain access not only to clinical information about a particular child, but also to social information about the child, including any previous child protection concerns. We discuss this issue in more detail in the final section of this chapter.

It is important to recognise the distinction made by Sidebotham (2003) between 'risk factors' and 'predictors' of abuse. Although injuries such as SDH in young children or spiral fractures (in long bones) have a high specificity to NAI and could consequently be used as predictors of abuse, *social* risk factors, such as a previous parental history of placement in local authority care, alcohol abuse or marital conflict, have a low specificity for abuse. Consequently, these social risk factors should not be used by health professionals as indicators of abuse but as signs that may warrant further discussion or opinion from colleagues in the relevant specialist areas. However, misconceptions still remain among doctors and other child protection professionals about the patterns of injuries in children who are physically abused. For instance, some medical professionals maintain that NAI in children is often a 'one-off' event or more likely to be caused by an accident. However, as we have pointed out, these views are increasingly being challenged by the research evidence, which shows that children who have been abused also display signs of prior abuse (Andronicus *et al.* 1998; Sanders *et al.* 2003). Moreover, children might present with physical injuries ranging from minor to severe in nature, and it is often difficult for clinicians to draw definite conclusions about the probable cause. For this reason, even if appropriate clinical investigations are conducted, the identification of NAI has to be made with reference to social risk factors, such as a previous history of abuse, or whether a carer has had a psychiatric illness. The tendency among health professionals has been to rely entirely on clinical investigations as a basis for identifying NAI. For example, a research study conducted for the National Society for the Prevention of Cruelty to Children (NSPCC) on the attribution of cause of child deaths in hospital settings found that social information was not given equivalent status to medical information as a matter of routine (NSPCC 2004).

Furthermore, recent media coverage of legal proceedings in suspicious baby deaths has frequently referred to the need to find a 'diagnosis' of child abuse, making the false assumption that child abuse or NAI is a clinical *diagnosis* (Dyer 2005a). References to 'diagnosing' abuse are also to be found in surveys designed to assess health professionals' perceptions of and ability to recognise physical child abuse, which include questions on the extent to which they can effectively 'diagnose' child physical abuse (Russell *et al.* 2004). However, this interpretation is largely misconceived. An injury is made up of a constellation of physical signs that can be given a clinical diagnosis, but an *injury* cannot be diagnosed as it necessarily implies a non-clinical cause, such as a physical trauma. The cause of the trauma itself is not amenable to a clinical diagnosis, but the physical signs that it displays are. Thus, the three clinical signs of shaking injuries (commonly referred to as the triad) are *diagnosable*. However, the cause of these injuries itself is *not diagnosable*, because this would imply that the social practice of child abuse could also be clinically diagnosed in the same way as a retinal haemorrhage or a rib fracture. This proposition suggests that the cultural expectation on medicine to find a 'diagnosis' of NAI in young children is misguided, and if current systems of identifying serious child abuse are to become more effective, child protection agencies will need to attach equal importance to the social evidence and the 'social' context of abuse.

The testimonies that are provided by carers following a traumatic episode are one such form of social evidence. However, the difficulty for paediatricians often lies in the balance that needs to be achieved between maintaining the trust of the carers, who may or may not be the suspects, without seeming to point the finger of blame. In many instances, referral decisions are made on the basis of interpersonal factors such as the outward appearance of the carers or the salience of their explanation for the injuries. Although all the relevant factors should be considered in such cases, the evidence nevertheless needs to be evaluated in a robust way so that the clinical signs as well as the non-clinical features are utilised in referral decisions. Consequently, this means that young children should undergo a comprehensive clinical assessment, and a thorough evaluation should incorporate a history provided by the carers and any social or criminal evidence that is available to the A&E doctor or the paediatrician. We return to this issue in the final section of this chapter.

The research literature does not support the proposition that all children have the same risk of abuse. Whitehead and Drever (1999) found that infant mortality is between 50 and 65 per cent higher in families who are in social class IV–V (partly skilled and unskilled) than in classes I–II (professional and managerial). Studies also show that mortality among babies of lone mothers is higher than in two-parent families, and poverty, young maternal birth age, low parental education and parental conflict were all positively related to a mother's use of physical punishment against the offspring (Kotch, Browne and Ringwalt 1995). Consequently, greater attention needs to be placed on the social, cultural and demographic characteristics of children (and the carers) who are admitted to hospital with physical injuries, to help in identifying suspected abuse, which cannot be diagnosed on the basis of clinical signs alone. The implications of this research evidence on the identification of NAI in children are highly significant.

Identifying non-accidental head injury in young children: the research evidence

One of the objectives of our research study was to identify factors which influence decisions to make a child protection referral when a young child is found to have sustained a SDH. Previous studies have examined the social characteristics of physically abused children and their carers, but much of the research has focused on sexual abuse (Felzen 2002) or non-specific physical injury (Sundell 1997) and only limited research has been conducted on babies and very young children. Investigations have also been conducted on the referral decisions of paediatricians, but these studies have focused predominantly on clinical factors predisposing clinicians to refer a suspected case of physical abuse (Jenny et al. 1999). To address the limitations of previous studies, our research sought to focus on the social context of very young children admitted to hospital with serious head injuries, which we hypothesised would provide a better profile of such cases, and offer clues as to the best way of identifying future episodes of suspicious head trauma. The study also provided data on the factors influencing clinical identification and referral of children to child protection agencies.

Physical child abuse is thought to be the commonest cause of a SDH in a young child (Jayawant et al. 1998; Kemp 2002). It was our hypothesis, therefore, that a large proportion (although the exact number is unknown) of children under two years of age admitted to hospital with a diagnosis of SDH will have been abused. At the time of the study, the belief among many child health clinicians was that a SDH was commonly caused by shaking a child, either with or without impact. The cause of a SDH was therefore believed to be traumatic ('external' rather than pathological). This belief was strengthened if the SDH was accompanied by the other two 'tell-tale' signs of NAHI; brain swelling and retinal haemorrhages (RH). Since the completion of the study, however, this hypothesis has been challenged by new research claiming to show that SDH in infants does not necessarily have a traumatic explanation. We discuss this in detail in Chapters 5 and 6, but it is now clear that each case is fact-specific. We therefore suggest that all cases of serious head trauma should be assessed individually, and caution should be exercised when a suspicion of NAI is raised. However, it is our belief, based on the research evidence in existence to date, that a non-accidental cause is more common in these cases than has been suggested by some proponents of the new research. Consequently, by drawing on our own findings, in the second part of this chapter we hope to show the problems inherent in the clinical identification of NAHI, and how a greater emphasis on social risk factors might help to improve the detection of such injuries.

Social characteristics of study sample

Our findings indicate that the sample of children who were referred to police and social services due to a clinical suspicion of NAHI were far from random, as has been the preconception in the past. The data show that the probability of a young child sustaining a serious head trauma was greater in 'materially deprived' families than in wealthier households, as determined by the Townsend Deprivation Index (Townsend, Phillimore and Beattie 1988). Our data also show that social problems such as alcohol and substance abuse, crime and violence within the household of our 54 children were especially evident. Of the 54 children who were referred to police or social services, 38 were male and 16 were female. Although our data paint an uncompromisingly negative picture of the social and material backgrounds of the children in our study, we believe that the findings offer opportunities for developing prevention strategies and health education campaigns that target carers whose children might be more vulnerable to traumatic head injury. However, as the analysis of the 14 children who were *not* referred to child protection agencies (discussed below) indicates, there is some evidence to support the 'selective referral' hypothesis, which states that health professionals are predisposed to referring children from 'deprived' backgrounds as they are perceived to be more at risk than children from wealthier households. Despite this, the selective referral hypothesis does

not explain all of the difference in clinical referral patterns. The large majority of our sample represented children who could be classified as materially
disadvantaged in comparison to the population average. Our field data support this assertion. The social services and police records provided detailed
descriptions of the socio-economic and lifestyle characteristics of the carers,
frequently referring to these households as 'disadvantaged' and 'materially
deprived'.

The social position of the mother, father and the mother's partner was
measured on the basis of their occupational status. This provided a broad
measure of social standing. Each parent or carer was categorised according
to their occupation at the time of the child's admission to hospital. The
occupational class is not an indicator of a parent's work history, and only
sought to provide a cross-sectional view of an individual's social position.
Most parents held jobs in unskilled, partly skilled and skilled manual professions, with a small proportion in professional, managerial or skilled
non-manual occupations. As indicated in Table 3.1, mental illness, drug and
alcohol abuse were relatively common among mothers and fathers. It is evident that in seven cases, mothers experienced physical abuse in childhood,
nine had post-natal depression following the birth of the (injured) child and
in nine cases the social services had registered previous care placements
against the carers. Not as many social problems were identified among
fathers and partners, possibly because a number of male carers were
remanded in custody on suspicion of abuse or had left the child's household
by the time of the case conferences or any subsequent child protection proceedings. This meant that accurate data on the social background of the
male carers were frequently unavailable.

The children lived predominantly in two-parent families. In total, 43
children lived with both natural parents, seven lived with their biological
mother and her partner, and four lived with the mother only. In 21 cases the
mother was married to and living with the birth father and in two cases the
mother was married to but not living with the birth father. The children
lived in a mixture of dwellings, although a large proportion resided in local
authority accommodation. In 23 cases the children lived in council accommodation, three in rented, and 11 in private dwellings. However, in 15 cases
the housing status of the child could not be identified from the records.

Table 3.1: Social history of carers (54 referrals)

Social history of carers	Mother	Father	Mother's partner
Mental illness	6 (11.1%)	5 (9.3%)	0
Drug abuse	3 (5.5%)	5 (9.3%)	1 (1.9%)
Alcohol abuse	3 (5.6%)	6 (11.1%)	0
Violence in current relationship	4 (7.4%)	3 (5.6%)	1 (1.9%)
Violence in previous relationship	2 (3.7%)	2 (3.7%)	1 (1.9%)
Physical abuse in childhood	7 (13%)	2 (3.7%)	0
Care in past	5 (9.3%)	2 (3.7%)	2 (3.7%)
Criminal record	4 (7.4%)	19 (35.2%)	5 (9.3%)
Post-natal depression	9 (16.7%)	N/A	N/A

Factors influencing referral to child protection agencies

The health professional taking responsibility for the child protection referral was usually a paediatrician. This is unsurprising given that the care of the child is usually transferred to the paediatrician following admission to hospital. Of the 54 children who were referred to social services, the referring clinician was a paediatrician in 42 cases, a community paediatrician in three cases, and in one case a neurosurgeon. The referring clinician in the remaining eight cases could not be identified from the files. Of the 54 children who were admitted to hospital, full or partial clinical investigations were conducted on 53 children based on the suspicion that they had suffered NAI (Table 3.2). The one case in which clinical investigations had not been conducted was also referred. Of the 53 children who had clinical investigations, 46 were confirmed as suspicious of NAI, three were considered equivocal and four cases were 'confirmed' as having a different cause such as a car accident or meningitis. However, they were all referred to police or social services.

Table 3.2: Consideration of NAI (54 referrals)

NAI considered	Frequency	Percentage
Yes (investigated/confirmed)	46	85.2
Yes (investigated/excluded)	4	7.4
Yes (investigated/equivocal)	3	5.6
Yes (not investigated)	1	1.9
Total	54	100

Of the 54 children with a suspected non-accidental SDH, 44 had coexisting injuries, most of which were considered to be non-accidental by the treating clinicians. In total, 25 children had fractures and 31 presented with bruising. Thirteen children had both fractures and bruising, and ten had no fractures or bruising. The data show that 36 children had RH, a sign which is strongly associated with a shaking injury. The findings also showed that 40 (74.1%) children who were referred to social services or police were less than six months old, which is consistent with other research. Fourteen children died following their injury, and the age distribution of deceased children was similar to that of the whole sample.

Medical opinion

Witness statements and reports were examined in the social services files to assess how far clinical opinion supported NAI as an explanation for the cause of the child's injuries. Statements were obtained from reports written by clinicians who either had direct contact with the child during admission to hospital, or who were invited to provide an expert opinion. The opinion of clinicians was grouped according to the degree to which they believed that the SDH was caused non-accidentally (for example, through shaking), where one represented definite NAI, and seven represented definitely not NAI.

Most clinicians believed that the child in respect of whom they were providing a statement of opinion was definitely, probably or possibly injured non-accidentally. In most cases paediatricians (either community or general) were asked to offer their opinions. Paediatric neurologists, neurosurgeons and radiologists also provided statements of opinion. It is unclear from the data, however, if paediatricians were more likely to offer a non-accidental explanation for the cause of the injuries than clinicians from different specialities because of the limited sample size. The data show that in 53 cases at least one medical opinion was obtained, in 41 cases two or more medical opinions were acquired, and in two cases five medical reports were obtained. In ten out of 54 cases there was conflict of opinion between clinicians as to the likely cause of the SDH. However, in 42 cases there was consensus of opinion. Much of the disagreement was due to the fact that some of the accidental explanations provided by the carers were thought to be clinically plausible. Also, in a few cases birth-related complications were considered to be a possible cause of the injuries, and it had been impossible to distinguish between a non-accidental and a clinical/accidental explanation. The data that were collected did not suggest that any conflict of opinion had been resolved. This is because most cases did not reach court (where conflicting opinion could be discussed) and medical reports were provided independently of each other, which meant that there was seldom any interaction between the authors of the medical reports to resolve conflicts of opinion. We discuss these issues further in Chapters 5 and 6.

Children with subdural haemorrhage who were not referred to child protection

There were 14 children in our study who were not referred to social services or police. Three of these children had died. Nine of the children were male and five were female, which is compatible with the age distribution of the 54 children who had been referred. In nine cases there was an explanation that was consistent with the clinical findings and further investigations and consideration of NAHI was not warranted (Table 3.3). There was major witnessed trauma in five cases (four road traffic accidents and one witnessed fall down stairs in the carer's arms). A subdural effusion was seen as a secondary complication of bacteriologically confirmed meningitis in two cases, in late

Table 3.3: Confirmed clinical diagnosis at admission (14 non-referrals)

	Major witnessed trauma	*Meningitis*	*Total*
Diagnosis	5	4	9

haemorrhagic disease of the newborn in one case and as a neuro-surgical complication in one case.

In a further five cases there were features that were *suggestive* of NAHI, although a joint investigation with social services was not undertaken (Table 3.4). For instance, in one case delayed complications of neuro-surgery were not thought entirely consistent with the procedure which had been undertaken six months previously. In two cases, explanations of household accidents by the carers were accepted despite neuro-imaging findings typical of NAHI (multiple SDH of different ages). Also, a further two cases with SDH were attributed to pneumococcal meningitis despite one being preceded by a basal skull fracture, where the only explanation was of a minor domestic trauma, and the other associated with a chronic SDH thought in retrospect to precede the infection (meningitis), which should have therefore raised a suspicion of NAI. The findings indicate that if all the available clinical and social evidence had been initially considered, the one case of delayed complications arising out of neuro-surgery, the two cases of household injury and the two cases of meningitis with haemorrhage should have been investigated further. These cases raise the question of how, and under what circumstances, a suspicion of NAI is raised and acted upon by paediatricians. This is a problem that requires further investigation.

In three of these cases NAHI was not considered, in one case the clinicians queried NAHI but did not conduct the necessary investigations, and in one case investigations were undertaken but no referral to social services was made. In conclusion, it is evident that in a significant proportion of children who presented to hospital with a SDH, no suspicion of NAI had been raised, where in hindsight the clinical evidence and the inconsistent explanations provided by the carer suggested a cause for concern. We are not arguing that all infants presenting with a SDH should be referred to child protection agencies, but that where sufficient uncertainty exists, more clinical tests should be conducted and greater multi-agency communication should be encouraged so that referral decisions are based on a thorough interdisciplinary assessment of the evidence.

The data also seem to indicate that there is a relationship between the age of the children and the probability of referral to child protection agencies. This seems to support the hypothesis that young children are at greater risk of shaking injuries. Table 3.5 illustrates the age and sex distribution of the 14 non-referrals. The median age of this group of children, eight

Table 3.4: Possible non-accidental cause of SDH (14 non-referrals)

Cause of SDH	Number of cases
Delayed complications of neurosurgery	1
Carers' explanations of accidents	2
SDH thought to be caused by meningitis	2
Total	5

Table 3.5: Age and sex of 14 non-referrals

Age (months) Mean 9.3 months	Female	Male	Total
2	1		1
3		1	1
5	1		1
7	1	1	2
8		3	3
10	1		1
11	1	1	2
14		1	1
15		1	1
21		1	1
Total	5	9	14

months (mean 9.3 months) is higher than the median age of the 54 children who were referred to child protection agencies (median three months). This is consistent with the theory that there is a higher risk of children under the age of approximately six months being shaken and suffering injury because they are lighter to pick up and they tend to cry more, which increases their vulnerability to these kinds of injuries.

We also examined the occupational status of the carers, which was largely representative of professional, managerial and technical occupations. Consequently, they represented a more affluent group than those whose children were referred to child protection agencies. Of the 30 parents that represent this group of cases, only 2 were unemployed. The housing status of the victims cannot be determined accurately because the data are incomplete, although it is evident that 5 of the 14 children lived in owner occupied households. The Townsend Deprivation Scores were calculated for the group of referred and non-referred cases, indicating that the level of deprivation among the former category was higher. A higher score represents a greater degree of deprivation (Townsend *et al.* 1988). The mean score for the 54 referred children was 0.86 and for the 14 who were not referred the score was −0.4814.

Table 3.6 illustrates the marital status of the mother in both the cohort of 54 children referred to police and social services and the cohort of 14 who were not referred. In the 54 referred cases, it is evident that the mother was just as likely to be married as not married. This is in contrast to the marital status of the mother in the cohort of the 14 cases which were not referred, where the mother was more likely to be married than not married. In nine out of 14 cases both parents were married, in three cases the mother was cohabiting with the father and in two cases the mother's marital status was unknown. The family composition of the 54 referred cases was more diverse than that of the 14 cases not referred, where the mother in the latter group was more likely to be cohabiting with a partner than living alone. However, this difference could equally be attributed to the smaller sample size. A larger sample might have elicited a similar pattern as that in the former group of referred cases.

Improving identification of non-accidental head injury

The only population based case series that has been conducted has suggested that the majority of SDH in children under two years of age are due to child abuse (Jayawant *et al.* 1998). This is supported by our research, which also identified a number of risk factors associated with NAHI injuries in very young children. The analysis of our research findings revealed that the children who sustained a suspected non-accidental SDH were likely to be under six months old, male, of a low socio-economic background and have a previous hospital admission since birth. The carers were likely to be in their late teens or early twenties (especially the mother), live in local

Table 3.6: Marital status of the mother

Marital status of mother (54 referrals)	Frequency
Single not living with bf	4
Cohabiting with bf	22
Married to bf, not living with him	2
Married to and living with bf	21
Separated from bf	4
Divorced from bf	1
Marital status of mother (14 non-referrals)	
Cohabiting with bf	3
Married to bf	9
Not known	2

bf = birth father

authority accommodation and were as likely to be married as unmarried. Also, drug and alcohol abuse was relatively common among the carers, as was a history of a placement in local authority care, physical abuse in childhood, post-natal depression of the mother and prior child protection concerns registered against the abused child or his/her sibling(s).

These findings contradict the views held by some researchers who claim that 'whiplash shaking' injury is independent of socio-economic factors (Becker et al. 1998; Caffey 1972). It is possible that our sample was partly determined by the selective referral practices of paediatricians and other clinicians. Factors such as socio-economic status, race, gender and perceived 'appearance' of the carers might play a significant part in affecting the perception of clinicians about the potential risk of abuse to a child. More research needs to be undertaken on this issue especially since our sample was not statistically representative, but other researchers have shown that clinical and social factors have a strong association with child abuse. For example, Jayawant et al. (1998) report in their study that a clear relationship exists between a SDH in a child under two years of age and the existence of fractures, other traumatic injury, retinal bleeding and a previous history of child abuse.

In our research cohort, 14 children were not referred to police and social services from the sample of 68. This was because the explanation offered by the carers was accepted and inconsistent clinical findings were ignored, or a medical cause was confirmed and a serious trauma had been witnessed. The data, however, do raise at least some questions about the criteria used by clinicians in their decision to investigate the possibility of NAI. For this, an ethnographic study would be particularly revealing. The data show that the background characteristics of the non-referred cases differed markedly from the 54 cases that were referred. For example, the occupational status of the parents was much higher in the group of non-referred cases, and the parents were relatively more likely to be married. Also, the median age of the children was higher (almost three times that of the 54 referred cases), which suggests that clinicians might have been less likely to investigate a non-accidental cause for the SDH in older children. The research served the purpose of illustrating a useful hypothesis, which states that a paediatrician's decision to refer a child to police or social services might, to some extent, be influenced by non-clinical factors such as the social and demographic characteristics of the carer(s). The socio-economic differences between the cases which were referred and those which were not suggest a need to research the social factors that might influence clinical referral decisions.

An urgent need exists to improve the training of clinicians in identifying NAHI in very young children, many of whom will present with coexisting injuries. Jayawant *et al.* (1998) found that a significant number of cases with a SDH did not receive a full clinical investigation, suggesting the strong possibility that vital coexisting features of abuse are being missed during the initial assessment. Kemp (2002) recommends that all young children who have a SDH diagnosed on admission to hospital where there is no clear underlying medical cause or history of witnessed major accidental trauma must have a series of essential baseline investigations, conducted by a multi-agency team including a paediatrician with expertise in child protection, a paediatric neurologist and/or neurosurgeon, a neuroradiologist, an ophthalmologist, social workers and police. The suggested assessments include:

- clinical history, including a full paediatric case history and full documentation of all possible explanations for the injury
- social and police history, including any previous child protection concerns and relevant criminal records of carers

- examination, including a thorough general examination, documentation and clinical photographs of coexisting injury and the monitoring of head circumference

- ophthalmology, including examination of both eyes using indirect ophthalmology through dilated pupils

- radiology, including initial cranial computerised tomography (CT) scan, repeat neuroimaging at seven and 14 days (magnetic resonance imaging (MRI) scan preferable), discussion of neuroimaging with neuroradiologist and full skeletal survey with repeat imaging at ten to 14 days

- serology, including full blood count repeated over first 24–48 hours, coagulation screen and urea and electrolytes, liver function tests and blood cultures.

The detailed investigation of young children presenting with an unexplained SDH, as recommended by Kemp, should minimise the number of abused children who remain undetected and, therefore, unprotected. However, the wider issue of child protection training for clinicians, particularly paediatricians, also needs to be addressed. In the past the availability of such training varied enormously across the country and was not mandatory. In January 2006 the Royal College of Paediatrics and Child Health and the NSPCC launched a new scheme which aims to give doctors more skills in managed suspected cases of child abuse (Royal College of Paediatricians and Child Health 2006). The training scheme: 'Safeguarding Children – Recognition and Response in Child Protection', is the first ever nationwide training course in child protection. It is to be rolled out to doctors training in paediatrics and will also be available to doctors working in A&E departments and GP surgeries. The introduction of the scheme is a significant step forward in child protection and it is hoped that the training will enable clinicians to be better equipped to recognise and respond to possible cases of child abuse. The course presents an ideal opportunity to encourage clinicians to be alert to the possibility of NAI and address the current culture of under-reporting. However, it is important that such training goes beyond highlighting clinical indicators of abuse and encourages a wider perspective by increasing awareness of the social risk factors that we have identified. It is also important that the training is supported by measures to address the growing reluctance of clinicians to engage with the child protection system. We explore this issue in detail in Chapter 6.

The research evidence suggests that closer inter-agency communication may foster a climate that is more conducive to the identification of children who have sustained a non-accidental SDH, and where referral decisions are based on all the available evidence. There is therefore a need for improved multidisciplinary collaboration between paediatricians, social workers and the police, so that information that might identify various risk factors is made more accessible to clinicians, and we suggest that further training of paediatricians should be conducted in conjunction with social workers, health visitors and the police, so that any subsequent assessment of risk incorporates a multi-professional perspective. For instance, the clinical identification of children who have sustained a non-accidental SDH could be improved if doctors had easy access to information relating to previous hospital admissions of the child and siblings; information from social work agencies on the carers such as previous child protection concerns, prior involvement with social services or alcohol and drug abuse; and police records that might identify further risk factors such as a criminal history of the carers. As we discussed in Chapter 1, following Lord Laming's inquiry into the death of Victoria Climbié (Laming 2003) and the implementation of the Children Act 2004, the roles and responsibilities of professionals who work with children have undergone radical changes which will inevitably impact on the way in which agencies work together. One of the key changes is the development of an Information Sharing Index, a development which has clear potential for improving the identification and reporting of suspected NAI. The precise scope of the information to be contained on the database will be determined by detailed regulations, but allowing A&E staff access to the Index will overcome the problems previously encountered in accessing local child protection registers. Even in the absence of any previously recorded child protection concerns, access to the Index could, dependent upon the information recorded, also alert the clinician to possible risk factors of abuse in individual cases. For example, Laming (2003) suggested that consideration should be given to extending the process of new child patient registration with GPs to include gathering information on wider social and developmental issues likely to affect the welfare of the child. The inclusion of such information on the Index would enhance the prospect of effective child protection.

In conclusion, we recommend that in all cases of serious physical injury in children under the age of two years, such as a SDH, skull fracture, major burns, scalds and related injuries, who present to an A&E department, a full clinical examination should be conducted. In addition, background checks should be made and a social history of the child and the carers should be taken to maximise the identification of children at risk of serious abuse. A&E doctors should not rely on subjective opinion or on issues of plausibility when making decisions about the cause of injuries to children. Although the focus on serious physical injury may detract from attention being directed at less serious injuries, an increased awareness of risk factors and access by A&E staff to social, as well as clinical, information will help to identify more children who are at risk of abuse. However, it must also be recognised that although detection of NAI can be significantly improved, the problems of differentiating between genuine accidental injuries on the one hand and abuse on the other still remain, and many children will inevitably slip through the net. Yet this should not prevent every effort being made to improve the system of identifying NAI in young children.

CHAPTER 4

Proving Non-Accidental Head Injury: From Mere Suspicion to Proof Beyond All Reasonable Doubt

In this chapter we begin by examining differing concepts of proof before moving on to a detailed analysis of the issues involved in proving non-accidental head injury (NAHI) in a young child. We explore the process of evidence building which takes place when a child protection referral is made and analyse the reasons for the attrition of cases as they progress through the child protection and criminal justice systems. Drawing on our research findings and recent legal and scientific developments, we then focus on the specific difficulties encountered in proving that a child has suffered NAHI in legal proceedings. We conclude by examining the potential for apparently conflicting outcomes in child protection proceedings and criminal prosecutions and consider the implications of this for effective multi-agency working.

The quest for truth and differing concepts of proof

According to the Oxford English Dictionary, 'to prove' something is to establish it as true; to make certain; to demonstrate the truth of by evidence or argument and 'proof' is that which makes good or proves a statement; evidence sufficient (or contributing) to establish a fact or produce belief in the certainty of something. Although of assistance in explaining the concept of proof, the usefulness of such definitions when considering whether non-accidental injury (NAI) has been proved is limited because an individual's understanding of terms such as 'make certain' and 'establishing facts' inevitably varies according to the context in which they are used.

Such variations in understanding are evident in the different terminology adopted when NAI is suspected. An individual may well hold a subjective belief that a child's injuries are non-accidental, but such a belief will not be sufficient to prove in any legal proceedings that the child has been abused. For example, a person who has concerns about the welfare of a particular child may claim to 'know' or 'be sure' that the child has suffered NAI. The evidence on which this state of mind is founded may vary considerably – from little more than an instinctive feeling to strong clinical indicators of abuse supported by independent corroborating evidence – but the individual's state of mind does not itself establish that the child has been abused. Guidance on inter-agency co-operation indicates that any person who believes or simply suspects that a child has suffered NAI, whether the belief or suspicion is formed in a personal or professional capacity, should refer their concerns to the local authority, the National Society for the Prevention of Cruelty to Children (NSPCC) or the police, all of whom have powers to intervene (Department of Health *et al.* 1999, para 5.6). Although any evidence gathered prior to a referral being made will be vitally important and may well form the basis of a subsequent finding that the injuries were non-accidental (particularly in the case of evidence recorded by the treating clinician), the child protection referral is the first step in the formal process of proving NAI and any belief in NAI formed prior to the commencement of this process cannot equate to the abuse having been proved.

In the following chapter, we examine the status that tends to be accorded to a clinician's belief in NAI and any medical testimony provided in court. This phenomenon is evident from the time the referral is made, particularly if the terminology used in making the referral is taken to indicate that the abuse has already been proved. One of the dangers inherent in multidisciplinary working is the potential for confusion and misunderstanding caused by conflicting professional ideologies and inconsistent use of terminology. As Mercier (1972) quoted in Bourne and Newberger (1979, p.142) explained:

> Each discipline is organised around a core of basic concepts and assumptions which form the frame of reference from which persons trained in that discipline view the world and set about solving problems in their field. The concepts and assumptions which make up the perspective of each discipline give each its distinctive character and are the intellectual tools used by its practitioners... Where the issues to be resolved are clearly in the area of competence of a single

discipline, the automatic application of its conceptual tools is likely to go unchallenged. However, when the problems under consideration lie in the interstices between disciplines, the disciplines concerned are likely to define the situation differently and may arrive at differing conclusions which have dissimilar implications for social action.

In cases of suspected child abuse, the disciplines involved have traditionally been categorised into three broad divisions: medical, legal and social, with each division tending to adopt its own professional ideology of the problem (Cobley 1995). However, advances in medical knowledge and resulting specialisation of medical science arguably now require finer distinctions to be made. For example, when Angela Cannings appealed against her conviction for murdering two of her children (which we discuss in detail in Chapter 6) evidence was received from a range of medical experts, including a consultant pathologist, consultant paediatric and perinatal pathologist, paediatric and perinatal epidemiologist, paediatric gastroenterologist, clinical physiologist, consultant cardiologist, immunologist and a microbiologist. As Wilson (2005) points out, a geneticist may well view a condition in a completely different way to a pathologist. Concepts of proof and truth may therefore differ both between and within the various disciplines and a clear understanding of the concept of proof and the issues involved in proving NAHI in a legal setting would undoubtedly facilitate effective multidisciplinary working.

The spectrum of proof following a child protection referral

Following a child protection referral, a multi-agency fact-finding process begins. One of the primary aims of this process will be to establish if the child's injuries are non-accidental so that action can be taken to protect the child and any other children in the family who may be at risk, and, where appropriate, to prosecute the person or persons responsible. However, the process of proving that a child has suffered NAI involves establishing past facts. Absolute certainty about events which happened in the past can rarely be achieved. Whilst this is true of all past events, whatever their nature, the problem is exacerbated in cases of suspected NAI to a child, which can be notoriously difficult to prove. In the absence of an unqualified admission by the abuser, the determination of facts can usually only be made to a degree of probability. Therefore references to 'making certain' and 'establishing as true' have to be qualified when applied to proving non-accidental injury. As Hedley J explained in the case of *A Local Authority v S and W and T* (2004):

> The truth is an absolute but elusive concept and the law, in recognising that, deals with it in terms of what can be proved. The fact that something cannot be proved does not mean that it did not happen but only that it cannot be proved to the requisite standard that it did. That is the price that society has to pay for human fallibility in the quest for truth. (para 8)

The degree of probability required to instigate, and then continue, state intervention in a child's life increases in stages during the fact-finding process, creating a spectrum of proof through which cases must pass in the quest for truth. When a child protection referral is first made, action may be taken on the basis of 'reasonable suspicion'. For example, a local authority have a duty to investigate whenever they have *reasonable cause to suspect* that a child who lives, or is found, in their area is suffering or is likely to suffer significant harm (Children Act 1989, s 47). Similarly, the police may arrest without warrant any person whom they have *reasonable grounds for suspecting* to be guilty of an arrestable offence (Police and Criminal Evidence Act 1984, s 24(6)). Although the courts have declined to quantify the degree of probability required to support the cause or grounds for reasonable suspicion, it is clear that it is relatively low and certainly does not equate to proving NAI. As Maurice Kay J explained in the case of *R v Hertfordshire County Council, ex parte A* (2001) 'there is a world of difference between satisfying a court that something is so…and having reasonable cause to suspect that it is so' (para 53).

As the fact-finding process continues, the degree of probability required to justify continued intervention in the child's life increases steadily. There are a variety of protective orders short of a full care order available under the Children Act 1989 which are triggered by *reasonable cause to believe* that the child is suffering or is likely to suffer significant harm. These orders include child assessment orders (s 43), emergency protection orders (s 44) and interim care orders (s 38). It is generally agreed that the requirement of reasonable cause to believe signifies a higher degree of probability than reasonable cause to suspect. It has even been suggested that, if there are ten steps from mere suspicion to a state of certainty, then reasonable suspicion may be as low as step two or three, whilst reasonable belief may be as high as step nine or ten (Bevan and Lidstone 1985, p.5). Although this arguably places reasonable cause to believe too close to certainty, it is at least clear that reasonable cause to believe still does not equate to proof of abuse – as Scott Baker J commented in *Re S (Sexual Abuse Allegations: Local Authority Response)* (2001) 'only when one comes to the full care order...does one find that allegations of maltreatment have to be *proved* on the balance of probability' (para 27 [emphasis added]).

The fact-finding process may eventually result in a court hearing, where the question of whether or not the child's injuries are non-accidental is ultimately determined by a court. This final determination may be made either during proceedings for a care or supervision order in the family courts, or following a criminal trial. However, in terms of probability, there exists a marked distinction between the different kinds of legal proceedings.

Care proceedings are civil proceedings and, in making a determination of fact, the court must be satisfied on the balance of probabilities. At its simplest, this means that the court must be satisfied that the child's injuries are more likely than not to be non-accidental. However, in cases involving serious allegations or having serious outcomes, judicial interpretations of the civil standard of proof have resulted in variations in the standard. Cases in which it is alleged that a child has suffered NAI are classic examples of such cases – they may involve allegations of serious crimes and may result in serious consequences such as the removal of a child from its family. Although there has been considerable confusion as to how the seriousness of a case should affect the standard of proof (Redmayne 1999), it now seems relatively clear that in cases involving allegations of child abuse, the courts adopt what is commonly referred to as the 'prior probability approach' (*Re H (Minors) (Sexual Abuse: Standard of Proof)* (1996) and *Re U; Re B* (2004)). This means that the standard of proof remains at the balance of probability, but the more serious the allegation, the less likely it is that it occurred and so the more cogent the evidence required to overcome the likelihood of what is alleged and thus to prove it.

In stark contrast to care proceedings, the degree of probability required to justify a finding of fact in criminal prosecutions is 'beyond all reasonable doubt'. Although there are problems surrounding the concept of 'reasonable doubt' it is at least clear that this is a very high standard. Indeed, the specimen direction approved by the Judicial Studies Board and which trial judges are encouraged to adopt refers to jurors being 'sure' of the defendant's guilt – a phrase which 51 per cent of prospective jurors interpreted to mean 100 per cent certain (Zander 2000).

There thus exists a spectrum of proof through which cases of suspected NAI must progress, as illustrated in Figure 4.1. At the outer limits of the spectrum, initial state intervention may be made on the basis of reasonable suspicion or belief. However, long-term intervention in a child's life can only be justified once the suspicion or belief has been proved in legal proceedings – either on the balance of probability in the family courts or beyond all reasonable doubt in the criminal courts. The centre of the spectrum – absolute certainty – is rarely, if ever, reached.

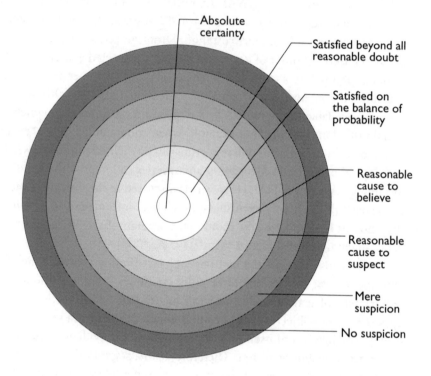

Figure 4.1: The spectrum of proof

The permissible use of evidence within the spectrum: from 'free proof' to 'controlled proof'

In forming a suspicion or finding a fact proved within the spectrum of proof, an individual must necessarily rely on some form of evidence to justify the suspicion or find the fact proved. At the outer limits of the spectrum when a child protection referral is made a system of 'free proof' (Twining 1990) operates whereby reliance can be placed on any available evidence in forming a suspicion. However, as cases progress through the spectrum increasing restraints are placed on the evidence which can be relied upon in determining facts, leading ultimately to a system of 'controlled proof' in the criminal courts, whereby the evidence on which the fact finder can rely is subject to strict controls (Roberts and Zuckerman 2004).

When a suspicion of NAI first arises, there are no legal restraints on the evidence which can be relied upon when deciding to make a child protection referral, although as a matter of logic any evidence relied on must be relevant to the possibility of NAI. An initial suspicion that a child is being abused may therefore be founded on virtually any available evidence, which may vary considerably in practice, ranging from concerns about the general behaviour or demeanour of a child (or indeed a suspected abuser) to visible evidence of injury to a child. Such free proof applies whether an individual is making the referral in a personal or professional capacity, although the evidence available to the referrer will depend on the context in which the initial suspicion is formed. For example, when conducting a clinical examination of a child, clinicians will rely primarily on their scientific knowledge and clinical expertise in identifying any injuries suffered by the child and forming a suspicion of NAI. However, as discussed in the previous chapter, clinicians will rarely rely exclusively on clinical information in forming a suspicion of NAI and, ideally, should take account of a wide range of evidence, including social factors (Sanders et al. 2003).

In the early stages of the multi-agency fact-finding process which follows the referral, the notion of free proof continues to apply. Although the requirement of a reasonable suspicion incorporates an objective test (as opposed to the subjective state of mind which suffices for a referral to be made), this does not of itself impose restraints on the evidence relied on in forming reasonable suspicion. Therefore at this stage in the spectrum, in theory at least, all professionals can rely on any available evidence. However, in practice there will inevitably be a tendency for those concerned with arrest and prosecution of the abuser to be influenced by the restraints which will be imposed on subsequent decision-making. Once a case involves the determination of facts by a court, there is a general requirement that the evidence relied on in court must be relevant to the fact or facts which are subject to proof. However, evidence is said to be relevant to a fact if it contributes towards proving or disproving a fact and so, in practice, the requirement of relevance will have been implicitly applied in the vast majority of cases from the time the initial suspicion was formed. In the family courts, where the welfare of the child is paramount, no further restrictions are placed on the admissibility of evidence. Indeed, the courts have stressed the importance of taking account of a range of evidence and have made it clear that, in care proceedings, in reaching conclusions on the issues before it the court should have regard to the 'wide canvas' of evidence available to it (*Re U; Re B* (2004)).

In stark contrast to the family courts, strict limits are imposed on the admissibility of certain kinds of evidence in criminal trials. The majority of these restraints are imposed on evidence on which the prosecution propose to rely in order to ensure that the defendant receives a fair trial as guaranteed by article 6 of the European Convention on Human Rights. Evidence may be excluded at a criminal trial because of the way in which it was obtained and these restraints must be borne in mind throughout the investigative process. For example, s 76 of the Police and Criminal Evidence Act 1984 provides safeguards against the admission of any confession made by the defendant which may have been obtained by oppression of the defendant or in consequence of anything said or done which was likely, in the circumstances existing at the time, to render unreliable any confession which might have been made by the defendant in consequence thereof. Furthermore, s 78 of the 1984 Act provides a general discretion for the court to refuse to allow evidence on which the prosecution proposes to rely to be given if it appears to the court that, having regard to all the circumstances, including the circumstances in which the evidence was obtained, the admission of the evidence would have such an adverse effect on the fairness of the proceedings that the court ought not to admit it. Evidence may also be excluded simply because of its nature or its likely prejudicial effect on the defendant.

Although the reasonable suspicion required to arrest a suspect may be based on any available relevant evidence, subsequent decisions must take account of these restrictions. For example, in deciding whether to charge a suspect, the Crown Prosecution Service (CPS) must be satisfied that there is a realistic prospect of conviction, and in deciding this, it must be considered whether the available evidence will be admissible in court and whether it is reliable (Crown Prosecution Service 2004). In the past one of the main restrictions related to evidence of the defendant's bad character. Traditionally, the defendant had what was colloquially known as a 'shield' which prevented the prosecution adducing evidence of, or cross examining the defendant about, his or her bad character. Although the protection was not absolute and in certain cases evidence of bad character would be admitted to show the defendant's propensity to act in a certain way and/or to attack his or her credibility, the prosecution was severely limited in the use they could make of evidence of the defendant's bad character. As a result of these restrictions, juries were frequently kept in the dark about a defendant's background when reaching a verdict. However, the Criminal Justice Act 2003 has now introduced a new regime which substantially widens the circumstances in which evidence of the defendant's bad character can be admitted. Irrespective of how a defendant runs his or her defence, evidence of bad character may now be admitted if it is relevant to an important matter in issue between the defendant and the prosecution. Such matters include the questions whether the defendant has a propensity to commit offences of the kind with which he or she is charged and whether he or she has the propensity to be untruthful. Thus, if a defendant charged with abusing a child has a history of violence, evidence of his or her background will now be admissible as part of the prosecution case, thereby making the prosecution's task of proving the abuse to the required high standard that much easier. However, despite the recent relaxation of certain restraints on admissible evidence, a system of controlled proof continues to operate in the criminal courts, thereby presenting a further barrier to the progression of cases through the spectrum of proof.

The attrition of cases of suspected non-accidental head injury through the spectrum of proof: the research evidence

As cases of suspected NAI proceed through the spectrum of proof there is an inevitable process of attrition as cases fail to progress to the next level of proof. This process was clearly evident as we tracked our cohort of research cases through the child protection and criminal justice systems and is illustrated in Figure 4.2. (More detailed information on the process of attrition is contained in the flow charts in the Appendix.) Although a child protection referral was made in 54 of the 68 cases which comprised the study cohort, only nine of these cases reached what is, in practice, the highest level of proof (beyond all reasonable doubt) and resulted in a criminal conviction. However one of these convictions was for neglect on the basis that the mother had failed to secure medical attention for her child and so NAHI was proven beyond all reasonable doubt in only eight cases. In care proceedings,

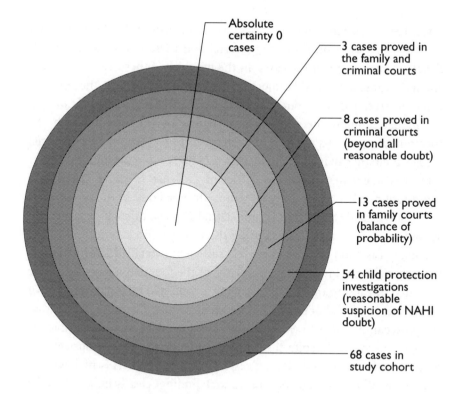

Absolute certainty 0 cases

3 cases proved in the family and criminal courts

8 cases proved in criminal courts (beyond all reasonable doubt)

13 cases proved in family courts (balance of probability)

54 child protection investigations (reasonable suspicion of NAHI doubt)

68 cases in study cohort

Figure 4.2: Proving NAHI: the attrition of cases in the study cohort

the threshold criteria for a care or supervision order were found to have been met (and NAHI thereby proved on the balance of probability) in 16 of the 54 cases (a criminal conviction had also been obtained in three of these cases). In the remaining 33 cases, no finding of NAHI was made in legal proceedings.

However, it is clear from the research findings that, although an inability to prove NAHI to the required standard was a factor in some of the cases which failed to progress through the spectrum of proof, it was by no means the *only* factor which contributed to the attrition of cases and it is therefore misleading to suggest that NAHI could not be proved in the 33 cases which did not result in a positive finding of fact by a court.

The attrition of cases in the criminal justice system

When tracking the cases through the criminal justice system there was found to be sufficient evidence to arrest one or more suspect in 34 of the 54 cases. Two of the remaining 20 cases were not considered to be NAHI after an initial investigation following referral and there was insufficient evidence to arrest in 18 of the cases. In the majority of these 18 cases, doubt about the cause of the child's injuries was a significant factor in the failure to make an arrest. However, once an arrest was made, the most significant factor in determining the subsequent progress of the case through the spectrum of proof was not lack of evidence as to *how* the injuries had been caused, but rather an inability to identify *who* had caused the injuries. Therefore, it is likely that there was sufficient evidence to prove NAHI in a significant number of the 21 cases which 'dropped out' of the system after an arrest was made but before a criminal trial. (Precise calculation is difficult as we lost track of seven cases during these stages and case records in the remaining cases did not always contain sufficiently detailed information on the reason for not proceeding.) Similarly, of the four defendants who were acquitted of causing the injury following a contested criminal trial (one of whom was convicted of neglect), three were acquitted because in each case the prosecution failed to establish that the defendant was responsible for causing the injury. Despite the current tendency to focus exclusively on problems relating to causation on cases of suspected NAHI (which we discuss in the following chapters), our research findings clearly indicate that, in practice, one of the main reasons for the attrition of cases through the spectrum of proof in the criminal justice system is the failure to identify the abuser, rather than an inability to prove NAHI.

The attrition of cases in child protection proceedings

A similar process of attrition was evident when tracking cases through the child protection system, although rather different factors tended to influence the decision-making process in these cases. A child protection conference was convened in 47 of the 54 cases. (NAHI had been discounted in one case following an initial investigation and six of the children had died before a conference could be convened.) Following the conferences, the child was placed on the child protection register in 38 cases, a further five children had died by the time the conference was convened, three children were deemed not to be at risk (because the suspected abuser had left the family home) and NAHI was discounted in one further case. Therefore, at the time of the child protection conference NAHI had been discounted in only two cases. (The cause of death in cases where the child had died from the injuries sustained was not established within the child protection system and the research found surprisingly little concern about potential risk to other children in the family – only one older sibling was made the subject of a carer order.) Following registration, a further three children died from their injuries, care proceedings were initiated in 16 cases and work was undertaken with the family on a voluntary basis in the remaining 19 cases. However, as we saw in Chapter 1, one of the principles underlying the Children Act 1989 is that local authorities should work in partnership with parents wherever possible and a court order should only be sought (and granted) if it would be better for the child than no order being made (Children Act 1989, s 1(5)). A failure to apply for a care order did not therefore mean that there was insufficient evidence to prove NAHI and it is likely that there was sufficient evidence to prove NAHI in many, if not all, of the 19 cases where work was undertaken with the family on a voluntary basis. Further support for this proposition can be derived from the fact that the research found a significant inverse association between the levels of co-operation of both the mother and the father and the decision to apply for a care order (Cobley 2004), suggesting that the parents accepted that the injuries were non-accidental in many of these cases.

Admissions and the attrition of cases

Denial of abuse by carers is commonplace. Wall J in *Re AB (Care Proceedings: Disclosure of Medical Evidence to Police)* (2002) commented that, in his experience, parental denial is both endemic and multi-factorial (para 81). Furthermore Lusk (1996, p.743) has argued that 'a predictable desire to avoid condemnation and possibly ostracisation by one's family, friends, employers and community is no less an incentive to deny culpability than the penalties of punishment and, perhaps, incarceration'. It is therefore not surprising that the research found a noticeable reluctance on the part of those suspected of abuse to admit responsibility for causing the child's injury. Although many carers were prepared to co-operate with social workers during the child protection investigation (and may thus have acknowledged responsibility at some stage), only four carers were prepared to admit responsibility at the first case conference and a further six carers subsequently admitted responsibility during the police investigation. Although arguably the admission in these ten cases can be equated with the NAHI having been proved, not all of these cases resulted in a finding of fact to this effect by a court. The research found that, in the child protection system, a care order was granted in only one of the four cases where an admission was made. (Two of the children had subsequently died, thus obviating the need for a care order and no order was deemed necessary in the final case.) In the criminal justice system, although all ten carers who admitted responsibility were charged with one or more criminal offences, we found that only six carers were subsequently convicted of an offence following a guilty plea. The research lost track of two of the ten cases due to the unavailability of some records. Of the remaining two cases, one carer retracted the admission before the case came to trial and the court ruled that the admission could not be admitted in evidence as it was held to have been obtained as a result of oppressive questioning by the police. In the final case the carer admitted in court that he had shaken his daughter, thereby causing her death, but he was acquitted of manslaughter as the jury were not convinced that the act of shaking was 'dangerous' in the sense required – an outcome that arguably highlights common perceptions of shaking in certain circumstances as we discuss later in this chapter.

The research therefore clearly indicates that, although an admission made during police investigations significantly increases the likelihood of conviction, an admission of responsibility will not necessarily result in a positive finding of fact by a court (Cobley 2004).

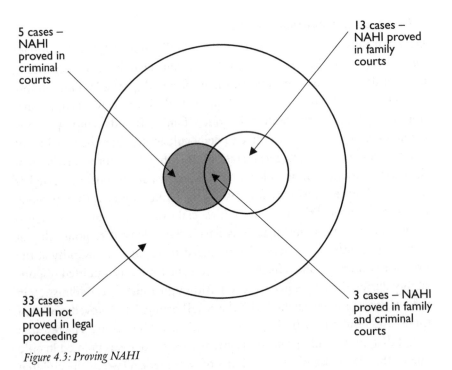

5 cases –
NAHI
proved in
criminal
courts

13 cases –
NAHI proved
in family
courts

33 cases –
NAHI not
proved in legal
proceeding

3 cases – NAHI
proved in family
and criminal
courts

Figure 4.3: Proving NAHI

How many cases were proved to be abuse?

The preceding analysis of the attrition of cases in the research cohort through the spectrum of proof shows that sufficiency of evidence to prove NAHI is only one of a number of factors which may influence the decision-making process. We can state with confidence that NAHI was proved in the 21 cases which resulted in the finding of fact by a court (either civil or criminal). However, although there was strong evidence to support the suspicion of NAHI in many of the remaining 33 cases (including, in some cases, an admission of abuse) and the failure of these cases to progress further through the spectrum may be attributable to a number of different factors, in the absence of a finding of fact by a court, NAHI cannot be said to have been proved in these cases.

Proving non-accidental head injury in legal proceedings

Having examined the spectrum of proof and the attrition of cases as they progress through the spectrum, we now turn attention to the specific difficulties encountered in proving disputed allegations of NAHI in proceedings for a care or supervision order and criminal prosecutions. In so doing we aim not only to provide a detailed analysis of current issues, but also to highlight the key distinctions between the two kinds of proceedings in order to explain the apparently inconsistent decisions which courts can reach in an individual case.

The facts to be proved and the burden of proof: who must prove what?

When an allegation of NAHI is disputed in court, the first key issue in determining the outcome of the proceedings will be to determine who must prove what facts. In legal proceedings, the general rule is that 'he who asserts must prove'. Therefore, in proceedings for a care order, the local authority have the burden of proving the required facts on the balance of probability. In criminal prosecutions, the prosecution generally bears the burden of proving the required facts beyond all reasonable doubt. In a limited number of cases, the defendant bears the burden of proving a defence, such as diminished responsibility (Homicide Act 1957, s 2(2)). When the defendant bears a burden of proof, he need only prove the facts on the balance of probability. The facts which must be proved depend on the nature of proceedings and, in criminal cases, on the specific offences charged.

The threshold criteria for care and supervision orders

As we discussed in Chapter 1, in child protection proceedings, where the primary concern is the welfare of the child, state intervention can only be justified on the basis that the child is suffering or is likely to suffer significant harm. For this purpose, harm is defined in s 31(9) of the Children Act 1989 as meaning ill-treatment or the impairment of health or development including, for example, impairment suffered from seeing or hearing the ill-treatment of another. Development means physical, intellectual, emotional, social or behavioural development, health means physical or mental health and ill-treatment includes sexual abuse and other forms of ill-treatment which are not physical. Although the legislation does not define 'significant', s 31(10) provides that, where the question of whether harm suffered by a child is significant turns on the child's health or development, his health or development shall be compared with that which could reasonably be expected of a similar child.

Although initial intervention will be justified on the basis of a reasonable suspicion or belief that the child is suffering, or is likely to suffer, significant harm, the court can only make a care or supervision order if it is satisfied on the balance of probability that the threshold criteria contained in s 31(2) of the Children Act 1989 have been met. These criteria contain a two-limb test. The court must first be satisfied that the child concerned is suffering or is likely to suffer significant harm. The second limb then requires the court to be satisfied that the harm, or likelihood of harm, is attributable to one of two alternative conditions: either the care given to the child, or likely to be given to him if the order were not made, not being what it would be reasonable to expect a parent to give to him; or the child's being beyond parental control.

Therefore, in cases of alleged NAI, the local authority will first need to prove that the child is suffering, or is likely to suffer, significant harm. The use of the term 'is suffering' is intended to concentrate attention on present or continuing conditions (Lyon *et al.* 2003) and the House of Lords has made it clear that the critical date for determining whether the child 'is suffering' significant harm is the date at which the local authority had initiated any protective action in order to safeguard the child (*Re M (Care Order: Threshold Conditions)* (1994)). The fact that the child has suffered harm in the past will not be sufficient to satisfy the threshold criteria, although past harm which is proved to the relevant standard will generally be sufficient to form the basis of a risk of future harm. However, an unsubstantiated allegation of NAI in the past cannot found the basis of a finding of risk of future harm. If there are concerns about siblings of an injured child, once the NAI has been proved to the relevant standard, intervention can be justified on the basis that the siblings are at risk of future harm. Once the harm has been proved, the local authority will then need to prove that harm, or likelihood of harm is attributable to the care given to the child, or likely to be given to him if the order were not made, not being what it would be reasonable to expect a parent to give to him. This inevitably raises questions as to *how* the injuries were caused and *who* inflicted the NAI.

Determination of the factual issues in order to satisfy the threshold criteria is only the first step towards the making of a care order. Once the threshold criteria have been satisfied, the court must then go on to satisfy itself that making an order would be better for the child than making no order at all. At this stage – commonly referred to as the welfare stage – the court will regard the child's welfare as its paramount consideration. The research findings indicate that, in cases of NAHI, once the threshold criteria have been met, the court is likely to make the order applied for in the vast majority of cases. In the research cohort, a care order was applied for and granted in 13 cases and two supervision orders were applied for and granted. A care order application was unsuccessful in only one case where, although the threshold criteria had been satisfied, by the time of the final hearing the order was not deemed necessary in the best interests of the child.

Criminal prosecutions: the substantive criminal law

In criminal prosecutions, the facts to be proved will vary according to the offence with which the defendant has been charged. The substantive criminal law will dictate the acts or omissions which need to be proved (formally referred to as the *actus reus* or external elements of the offence), the level of culpability required (formally referred to as the *mens rea* or fault element of the offence) and any defences which may be applicable. The actual offence charged and defences raised will depend on the nature of the alleged NAI. In cases where the child has died as a result of the abuse, the appropriate charge will be one of the common law offences of murder where there is evidence of an intention to kill or cause grievous bodily harm (GBH) (serious injury), or manslaughter if the required intention cannot be proved. All that is required for manslaughter is that the defendant commits an unlawful act which is dangerous in the sense that it is such that all sober and reasonable people would inevitably recognise must subject the child to, at least, the risk of some harm resulting, albeit not serious harm (*R v Church* (1966)). If the deceased child was under the age of 12 months and the defendant is the child's mother, a charge of infanticide may be brought under s 1 of the Infanticide Act 1938. Although there are very few convictions for infanticide each year (and there were none in our research cohort), the offence of infanticide has been the subject of considerable debate, not least because it is based on the belief that the ordinary conditions of childbirth and lactation have a potentially disruptive effect on mental state and behaviour of women. However, it does appear to be a useful tool to ensure lenient sentences for some women who kill their young children, who are viewed as tragic cases (Mackay 1993). Where the child survives, the defendant may be charged either with an offence involving GBH or actual bodily harm (ABH) under ss 18, 20 and 47 of the Offences Against the Person Act 1861, or with the offence of wilfully ill-treating or neglecting a child in a manner likely to cause unnecessary suffering under s 1 of the Children and Young Persons Act 1933.

A defendant charged with murder following the death of a child may raise the issue of diminished responsibility or provocation, both of which act as a partial defence reducing the conviction from murder to manslaughter. In order to succeed in a plea of diminished responsibility, s 2 of the Homicide Act 1957 requires the defendant to prove that he was suffering from an abnormality of the mind which substantially impaired his mental responsibility for his acts. Although the defence applies to both men and women, research has shown that, in relation to parents who kill their children, women are far more likely to be dealt with on the basis of diminished responsibility (Wilczynski and Morris 1993). Section 3 of the 1957 Act provides that, where there is evidence on which the jury can find that a person charged was provoked (whether by things done or things said or by both together) to lose his self-control, the question whether the provocation was enough to make a reasonable man do as he did shall be left to be determined by the jury; and in determining the question, the jury shall take into account everything both done and said according to the effect which, in their opinion, it would have on the reasonable man. The potential scope of a plea of provocation is wide. For example, the Court of Appeal held in *R v Doughty* (1986) that the persistent crying of a young baby falls within the scope of 'things said or done', and that, if there is evidence on which the jury may find that the crying had caused the defendant to lose self-control, then the issue of provocation should be left to the jury.

The facts to be proved: the major hurdles in cases of non-accidental head injury

Although difficulties may be encountered in proving each of the relevant facts in any particular case, drawing on our research finding and subsequent events it is possible to identify three main areas of difficulty in cases of NAHI: proving the cause of the child's injury or death; identifying the perpetrator and establishing the culpability of the person responsible for causing the injuries. Although the first of these issues was not found to be unduly problematic in the cases in the research cohort, further scientific research has resulted in a storm of controversy and the issue of causation and the provision of expert medical evidence thus merits detailed consideration in Chapters 5 and 6. Consideration is given to the remaining two issues below.

Who did it? Identifying the perpetrator in cases of non-acidental head injury

Once the court is satisfied that a child has suffered NAI, consideration must then be given to the question of who caused the injuries. The research findings indicate that the question of *who* caused the injuries (as opposed to *how* they were caused) is frequently the most difficult issue to prove in cases of NAHI (Cobley, Sanders and Wheeler 2003). This may be because the timing of the injury cannot be established with any precision and the child may have been in the care of a number of different carers throughout the window of opportunity. Alternatively the child may have been in the care of two (or more) people when the injury was inflicted and it cannot be determined which carer was responsible. Whilst it is obviously desirable to identify the abuser wherever possible, a failure to do so has very different consequences in criminal prosecutions and child protection proceedings.

Identifying the perpetrator in criminal prosecutions

In criminal prosecutions, if the child was in the care of two or more carers during the period when the injury was inflicted, traditionally no carer could be convicted of causing the injury unless it could be proved that all carers were present when the injuries were inflicted and actively participated in the abuse, or that one failed to intervene to protect the child (and is thus liable for aiding and abetting the assault) (*Lane v Lane* (1985)). The only alternative charge would be one of cruelty or neglect under s 1 of the Children and

Young Persons Act 1933, which does not require proof of an assault and can be based on a culpable failure to obtain medical assistance for the injured child. The research found that it was common practice for the prosecution to use the offence of neglect as a 'fall-back' offence on which the prosecution could rely if the defendant was not convicted of causing the actual injury to the child. The indictment included the offence of neglect in 5 out of the 13 cases which proceeded to trial. In four of these cases, the offence of neglect was left on file (i.e. was not proceeded with) when the defendant was convicted of causing the injury to the child. In the one remaining case the mother was acquitted of all charges of assault on the child, but was convicted of the offence of neglect on the basis that she had not sought medical attention for the child as soon as reasonably practicable.

In the early stages of an investigation it is common for two or more individuals to be under suspicion for injuring the child and two or more individuals may be arrested in any one case. For example, the research found that a total of 106 individuals were suspected of having injured the child in the 52 cases where NAHI was suspected following an initial investigation (Table 4.1) and both carers were arrested in 17 cases. However, because of the difficulties frequently encountered in identifying the perpetrator, joint charges are more rare and joint convictions even more so. Joint charges were brought in only four cases in the research cohort. Two of these cases were discontinued by the CPS after charge on the grounds that there was insufficient evidence to secure a conviction as the perpetrator could not be identified. Only one of the remaining cases proceeded to trial where the father was convicted of manslaughter and the mother was convicted of neglect.

Table 4.1: Suspects, arrests and charges

Suspect	Initially suspected	Arrested	Charged
Father	45	25	17
Mother	52	20	8
Mother's partner	7	5	3
Childminder	2	1	1
Total/number of cases	106 in 52 cases	51 in 34 cases	29 in 25 cases

The difficulties encountered in identifying the perpetrator are by no means unique to our research. Between 1997 and 2000, police forces in England and Wales dealt with 492 cases where a child had been unlawfully killed or seriously injured by their parents or carers. Of the 366 completed investigations, a total of 225 (61%) led to no charge at all and only 141 (39%) reached a criminal trial. The final conviction rate was 27 per cent. In contrast the conviction rate where a child is killed by a stranger, as opposed to a parent or carer, is 90 per cent (NSPCC 2002). In 2002 the NSPCC set up a working group as part of its Full Stop campaign to discuss how the law and procedures could be changed to ensure that parents and carers who kill or seriously injure their children can be brought to justice. The group held a conference in November 2002 and the case studies presented at the conference reflect many of the scenarios encountered in our research: Angus, a six-month-old child, was found lifeless in his cot. His parents denied harming him. The coroner recorded a verdict of unlawful killing and went as far as to say he was convinced the parents were lying and he was 'fairly confident' which of them had shaken Angus to death. No charges were brought against the parents. Emily was 15 months old when she died of brain damage caused by violent shaking. Her parents would not say what had happened to their child. The coroner returned a verdict of unlawful killing. Although the parents were the only adults in the house neither faced murder or manslaughter charges through lack of evidence. Chloe was four months old when she died from severe head injuries. Her parents blamed each other. At their trial the judge directed the jury to find them not guilty of murder as it could not be proved which of them dealt the fatal blow (NSPCC 2002).

The inability to convict either carer of actually causing the injury in such cases has been increasingly seen as a major source of injustice. The efforts of the NSPCC working group highlighted the issue which was also considered by the Law Commission the following year (Law Commission 2003). Recommendations for change have now been partially enacted in the Domestic Violence, Crime and Victims Act 2004, which introduces a new offence of causing or allowing the death of a child or vulnerable adult. Section 5 of the Act provides that members of a household who have frequent contact with a child under the age of 16 (or certain vulnerable adults) will be guilty of an offence if they caused the death of that child or if three conditions are met: first, they were aware or ought to have been aware that the child was at significant risk of serious physical harm from a member of the same household; second, they failed to take reasonable steps to prevent the child coming to harm and, finally, that the child subsequently dies from the unlawful act of a member of the household in circumstances that the defendant foresaw or ought to have foreseen. Thus the offence may be applicable in two different circumstances – the defendant may have caused or allowed the death of the child – but the prosecution do not have to prove which of the two circumstances apply to the defendant.

It is anticipated that only a small number of charges will be brought under the new provisions, which were brought into force in March 2005 (Home Office 2005). The Law Commission had recommended that there should be a statutory statement of responsibility applicable to those responsible for the child at the time he or she was killed. This would have encouraged suspects to provide information and potentially allow adverse inferences to be drawn at trial from a suspect's silence during police questioning, but the recommendation is not contained in the 2004 Act. The Law Commission had also recommended that the new offence should extend to children who are seriously injured, thereby protecting a far wider number of victims of abuse. However, the offence as enacted applies only where the child has died as a result of abuse. As Hayes (2005) points out, although there are some positive aspects of the new provisions, such as the message to householders that they have a duty to protect a child from a lethal assault perpetrated by another member of the child's household, the provisions are also a missed opportunity because they do not adequately reflect the Law Commission's suggested reforms. Just weeks after the new provisions were brought into force, media attention focused on the case of Michelle Oates and Adam Duke, who admitted neglect after a toddler in their care received serious injuries. It was found that the injuries were non-accidental and must have been caused by Oates or Duke (or both of them) but, as neither admitted responsibility, both could only be convicted of the lesser charge of neglect and were sentenced on the basis that they did not cause the injury and did not know the full extent of the injuries until the child was in hospital (*The Times*, 16 April 2005). The case immediately led to calls from children's charities for the law to be reviewed. In the meantime, although fewer carers may be able to literally get away with murder, cases of the 'which one of you did it' kind, where the child survives, will continue to pose significant hurdles for the prosecution.

The uncertain perpetrator and child protection proceedings

Although the inability to identify an individual perpetrator is frequently an insurmountable hurdle in criminal prosecutions, it would clearly be unacceptable if the state could only intervene to protect a child if an individual perpetrator could be identified. If it is alleged that a child has been injured while in the joint care of his or her parents, it is clear that the local authority does not have to prove which of the parents was responsible in order for the threshold criteria to be satisfied, either in relation to the injured child or any uninjured siblings. As Wall J commented in *Re CB and JB (Care Proceedings: Guidelines)* (1998) 'To hold otherwise would…not only be illogical, but would render the statutory provisions ineffective to deal with a common-place aspect of child protection' (p.249). However, the Court of Appeal has stressed that it is in the public interest to identify, wherever possible, the person responsible for inflicting the injury as children, when they grow up, have a right to know who injured them, rather than being forced to assume that both parents were responsible (*Re K (Children) (Non-Accidental Injuries; Perpetrator: New Evidence)* (2004)).

Cases in which the possible perpetrators extend beyond the immediate family and include, for example, childminders, tend to raise rather more difficult issues. In the case of *Lancashire County Council v B* (2000) a young child had suffered serious head injuries. During care proceedings, the judge found as a fact that the child had been violently shaken on at least two occasions and that the person responsible was either the mother or father, or the childminder who cared for the child on a regular basis. However, on the available evidence the judge could not determine which of three possible perpetrators was responsible for inflicting the injuries, all three making 'less than satisfactory witnesses'. The judge therefore concluded that the second limb of the threshold test – i.e. that the harm was attributable to the care given to the child – had not been established. The Court of Appeal reversed the judge's decision, and the decision of the Court of Appeal was upheld by the House of Lords. Lord Nicholls explained that the phrase 'care given to the child' refers primarily to the care given by a parent or parents or other primary carers. However, he went on to say that in a case of shared caring where the court is unable to identify which of the carers provided the deficient care, the phrase was apt to embrace the care given by *any* of the carers (p.147), which means that the threshold criteria can be established where there was no more than a possibility that the parents were responsible for any injury suffered by the child. Although the outcome of this case is generally regarded as the 'right' one, which ensures that the local authority can take appropriate protective action in cases involving uncertain perpetrators, the approach adopted by the House of Lords to arrive at this outcome has been criticised. Rather than relying on a purposive construction to the phrase 'care given to the child' in cases of shared care where an individual perpetrator cannot be identified, it has been suggested that a preferable approach in such cases would be to base the proceedings, and the legal analysis, on the alternative ground of risk of future harm (Hayes 2004). It is clear that the appropriate test to be applied when considering whether a child is likely to suffer significant harm is that of a 'real possibility' (*Re H (Minors) (Sexual Abuse: Standard of Proof)* (1996)). Although the majority of the House of Lords has held that the real possibility must be established on the basis of proven facts, in uncertain perpetrator cases where it is clear that the child has been injured this requirement will pose no difficulty. As Hayes (2004) points out, an analysis based on whether there was a real possibility of future harm to the child would more fairly have reflected the true position in the *Lancashire* case, namely that attribution to the parents of the child's past harm might be entirely wrong, but that the level of risk to the child if the parents were, indeed, the perpetrators of that harm demanded that the court had power to intervene and power to impose some type of protective order.

In the same case, the local authority had also sought a care order in relation to the childminder's own child, who was the same age as the injured child but who had not suffered any injury. The judge, having found that the threshold criteria could not be established in relation to the injured child, inevitably concluded that they could not be established on the basis of future harm in relation to the childminder's child. The Court of Appeal upheld this decision, stating that the risk of future harm could only be established on the basis of proven facts and, as it had not been established that the childminder was responsible for shaking the injured child, there was nothing on which to establish the risk of future harm. No further appeal was taken on this point, but the reasoning of the Court of Appeal has been criticised. Perry (2000) has argued that the 'fact' which must be proved in order to establish that a child is likely to suffer significant harm is the fact of significant harm having been suffered, rather than the precise identity of the perpetrator of that harm. In her view, confusion between the importance of proof of the fact of harm itself and the identity of the perpetrator of the harm led the Court of Appeal to reach the wrong conclusion on this point. Furthermore, as both Perry and Hayes (2000) point out, if the injured child had had a sibling who had not been injured, the Court of Appeal's reasoning would mean that the threshold criteria could not be established in relation to the sibling – an outcome which is deeply worrying.

The House of Lords has subsequently made it clear in *Re O and N (non-accidental injury): Re B (A Child) (non-accidental injury)* (2003) that, where the evidence at the threshold stage is not sufficient to exclude either parent as the perpetrator, it would be wrong to proceed on the basis that a parent had been found not to be the perpetrator. As a consequence, in cases involving an uncertain perpetrator, having found the threshold criteria to be established, the case should proceed on the assumption that each parent is a *possible* perpetrator. Following this decision, in *North Yorkshire CC v SA* (2003) the Court of Appeal held that the appropriate test in determining the pool of possible perpetrators is whether there is a 'likelihood or real possibility' that a particular person or persons was the perpetrator or a perpetrator of the inflicted injuries.

Non-accidental head injury and culpability

Once the perpetrator, or possible perpetrators, have been identified, it must then be proved that their behaviour was culpable. Whereas child protection proceedings are not concerned primarily with attributing blame, in stark contrast the function of criminal prosecutions is to impose sanctions on those who have committed a criminal offence. Thus, there are marked differences in the level of culpability required in the two kinds of proceedings.

Fault in the criminal law: intention, recklessness and neglect

The level of culpability required in a criminal trial is dependent on the offence charged. The offences of murder and causing GBH with intent under s 18 of the Offences Against the Person Act 1861 are offences of specific intent which require the prosecution to prove that the defendant either intended to kill the child or to cause the child GBH. In contrast, the offence of manslaughter, offences of inflicting GBH under s 20 and assault occasioning ABH under s 47 of the 1861 Act and the offence of wilfully assaulting, ill-treating or neglecting a child under s 1 of the Children and Young Persons Act 1933 can be satisfied by proof of recklessness or, in the case of s 1 of the 1933 Act, negligence. Offences of specific intent are therefore more serious offences and carry a heavier maximum penalty. Proving intention can be notoriously difficult in the absence of a confession. It is clear that a result is intended when it is the defendant's purpose to cause it, but in many cases the defendant may claim it was not his purpose to injure the child, or even that he did not foresee that his actions would result in the injury sustained. Following the judgement of the House of Lords in *R v Woollin* (1999) a court or jury may also find that a result is intended, even though it is not the defendant's purpose to cause it, when the result is a virtually certain consequence of the defendant's act and the defendant knows this to be the case. Therefore the defendant who throws a crying baby across a room in a fit of temper may be found to have intended the resulting injuries, even if it was not his purpose to cause them.

However, the research findings suggest that proving intention is frequently an insurmountable hurdle in cases of NAHI, or at least one which the prosecution avoid facing where possible by reducing charges to those which can be satisfied by proof of recklessness. Police initially brought charges against 29 suspects in 25 cases. Male carers were almost three times as likely to be charged as the mother.

As Tables 4.2 and 4.3 show, the police charged suspects with offences of specific intent in 56 per cent of the cases where a charge was brought and 85 per cent of the defendants facing trial on indictment had initially been charged with offences of specific intent. However, at the time of the trial, the indictment contained an offence of specific intent in only four cases (30%). In two of these cases the prosecution accepted a guilty plea to a lesser charge at the start of the trial. The remaining two defendants (one indicted for murder and one indicted for s 18) were both acquitted following a contested trial. Thus no convictions were obtained for offences of specific intent.

At first sight the number of reduced charges and the absence of convictions for offences of specific intent were surprising, particularly given the serious injuries sustained by many of the victims. Unfortunately, the unavailability of CPS records meant that it was not possible to investigate the reasons underlying the CPS decisions to reduce charges from ones of specific intent to ones which can be committed recklessly or negligently. Nor do the two cases where a charge of specific intent was successfully defended throw much light on the matter. The murder charge resulted in a directed acquittal at the end of the prosecution case after the judge ruled that similar fact evidence on which the prosecution proposed to rely was inadmissible and the jury acquitted a mother of charges under s 18 of the

Table 4.2: Initial charges brought by police (only the most serious charge is listed for each suspect)

Suspect	Murder	Manslaughter	s 18	s 20	s 47	s 1	Total
Father	2	3	6	4	1	1	17
Mother's partner	1			1		1	3
Mother			4	3		1	8
Childminder			1				1
Total	3	3	11	8	1	3	29

1861 Act after the judge ruled that her confession was unreliable and therefore inadmissible.

Despite a lack of hard evidence from the research findings, it is suggested that the difficulty in proving intent may be attributed to two factors. The first is doubt about the degree of force required to cause the injuries, controversy over which we discuss in detail in Chapter 5. The second factor relates to commonly held perceptions of shaking as a mechanism for causing NAHI.

Culpability and the degree of force required

Although this issue was not specifically raised in any of the cases in the research cohort, there is clear evidence from decisions of the Court of Appeal that this is a crucial issue in proving specific intent where the allegation is that the injuries were caused by the child having been shaken. In the case of *R v Stacey* (2001) a childminder had been convicted of murder after a six-month-old child in her care died after suffering NAHI in the form of bilateral subdural haemorrhage (SDH) and damage to the eyes. At her trial it was common ground that the injuries had been inflicted by shaking the child. On appeal, the Court of Appeal was troubled by the question of whether the jury was entitled to find she intended to do really serious harm to the child. The court pointed out that although an intent to do serious bodily harm may be quickly formed and soon regretted, so may a less serious intent, simply to stop a child crying by handling him in a way that any responsible adult would realise would cause serious damage or certainly might do so, which would only provide the mental element necessary for

Table 4.3: Charges, indictments and outcomes of cases which proceeded to trial (only the most serious charge is listed for each suspect)

Defendant	Initial charge	Charge on indictment	Plea	Verdict
Father	Murder	Murder	G to manslaughter – accepted by prosecution	G
Mother	Neglect	Neglect	G	G
Father	Murder	Manslaughter	NG	NG
Mother's partner	Murder	Murder	NG	Directed acquittal
Father	Manslaughter	Manslaughter	NG	G
Father	s 18	s 20	G	G
Father	s 18	s 1	G	G
Father	s 18	s 20	G	G
Father	s 18	s 20	G	G
Mother	s 18	s 20	G	G
Mother	s 18	s 18	G to s 20 – accepted by prosecution	G
Mother	s 18	s 18	NG	NG
Mother	s 18	s 20	NG	NG (G of neglect)
Father	s 47	s 47	Prosecution offered no evidence at trial	Directed acquittal

manslaughter. Being unable to discern anything which, in its judgment, would have made it safe to convict the childminder of murder, the court set aside the conviction and substituted a conviction for manslaughter. A similar outcome was reached several years later in the case of *Rock*, one of four conjoined appeals heard by the Court of Appeal which we discuss in detail in Chapter 6 (*R v Harris and others* (2005)). In this case the Court of Appeal concluded that a brief period of violence (going beyond even rough play) was all that was required to cause the child's fatal injuries and that, although such evidence undoubtedly furnished the mental element necessary for a conviction of manslaughter, it did not necessarily demonstrate an intention to cause serious harm, which was required for a murder conviction to be upheld. The Court therefore quashed Rock's conviction for murder and substituted a conviction for manslaughter. Similar considerations apply to those charged with causing GBH with intent where the child survives.

Perceptions of shaking

The second factor which exacerbates the difficulties of proving intention is commonly held perceptions of shaking as being distinct from other forms of child abuse. Indeed, perceived reduction in culpability of a defendant may even result in a complete acquittal. This was evident in one case in the research cohort where a father had admitted shaking his daughter and causing her death. The jury acquitted him of manslaughter after seeking guidance from the trial judge on the fault element required, thereby appearing to decide that the act of shaking was not 'dangerous' in the sense required. However, as juries are not required to give reasons for their verdicts, such blatant examples of perceptions of shaking will be rare. Furthermore, in recent years high profile prevention campaigns (NSPCC 2001; NSPCC 2003) and the resulting heightened awareness of the dangers of shaking a young child should impact on jury decision-making in future cases. By 2005 Rose J in the *Attorney General's Reference (No 16 of 2005)* (2005) was of the opinion that 'most parents of small babies are aware that shaking may cause a brain injury'.

A more fruitful source of evidence on perceptions of shaking can be found during the sentencing process which follows conviction. Although the small number of cases in the research cohort which reached this stage makes it difficult to draw any firm conclusions from the research itself, a review of sentencing comments made by the Court of Appeal over the last decade cast an interesting light on the judiciary's perceptions of shaking and the culpability of defendants. In the case of *R v Scott* (1995), the defendant pleaded guilty to inflicting GBH on his four-week-old son by shaking him and was sentenced to two years' imprisonment. The Court of Appeal reduced the sentence to 12 months and Kay J explained:

> it is necessary to go on and look at the particular acts that resulted in the injuries that this poor child suffered. They were not blows. They were not offences of throwing the child to the floor, or against some object as this Court sometimes has to consider. They were simply shaking a child and shaking a child in circumstances where the appellant, an otherwise loving father, was finding it difficult to cope with a very young baby. (p.452)

Whatever sympathy the Court may have felt for the appellant, those concerned with campaigns to prevent NAHI by educating carers on the dangers of shaking a baby will undoubtedly be horrified by the phrase '*simply* shaking a child', particularly when used in the context of an authoritative judgement from the Court of Appeal.

Comments were made in a similar vein two years later in the case of *R v Graham* (1997). The defendant pleaded guilty to inflicting GBH on his six-month-old son by shaking him and was sentenced to two and a half years' imprisonment. On appeal the Court of Appeal reduced the sentence to two years' imprisonment, suspended for a period of two years. Schiemann J commented:

> It is perfectly clear from the facts of this case that the injuries done to the boy were done in circumstances when this appellant was just dead tired and aggravated by a screaming child, a very common phenomenon for parents, and this is not one of these cases which unfortunately come before this court when a defendant has apparently got some psychological satisfaction out of battering a defenceless child. (p.266)

Whilst this comment may have been slightly more understandable if the case involved an isolated incident of shaking, when the child was admitted to hospital there was evidence of SDH of two different ages, and bony injuries involving his femurs, both upper arms, the left shoulder, one rib and the lumbar spine which had been caused on three separate occasions – hardly an isolated incident of shaking by a father who was '...*just* dead tired and aggravated by a screaming child'.

A further indication of the Court of Appeal's perception of shaking was given in *R v Hulbert* (1998) the following year. Hulbert admitted shaking his four-week-old daughter on two or three occasions, causing two SDHs of different ages and rib fractures. He pleaded guilty to two counts of inflicting GBH and was sentenced to nine months' imprisonment on each count, to be served concurrently. On appeal, the Court of Appeal referred to the case of *Graham* and suspended the term of imprisonment. In giving judgement the Court accepted the view of counsel for the defendant that shaking could be distinguished from a blow or blows because shaking was said to be '...an involuntary expression of the exasperation that no parent has not at some stage or another felt when a child reacts, as this child did, on this occasion' (para 13). Although the reference to the child's 'reaction' is puzzling (the only evidence being that the baby had cried – something which can hardly be described as a 'reaction' from a four-week-old baby) this comment amounts to an express recognition of what may be referred to as an attitude akin to 'there but for the grace of God go I'. These comments provide ample evidence that even the judiciary have tended to perceive shaking as distinct from other forms of child abuse. We can only surmise that such emotive reactions to shaking as a mechanism for causing NAHI in young children have influenced decision-making at all stages of an investigation, with the attendant dangers of inappropriate action being taken.

Fault and the defence of reasonable chastisement

Even if the prosecution can establish the necessary culpability of the defendant, in non-fatal cases the defendant may raise the defence of reasonable chastisement. In *R v Hopely* (1860) it was confirmed that moderate and reasonable punishment may be used by a parent or someone acting on behalf of a parent to 'correct what is evil in a child', as long as such punishment was not excessive or protracted. What amounts to reasonable chastisement became increasingly controversial during the late twentieth century, with other European countries imposing outright bans or limiting the use of corporal punishment of children (Booth 2005). Matters came to a head in the UK in 1998. A father had beaten his nine-year-old son on more than one occasion with a garden cane, causing bruising, and was charged with assault occasioning ABH. He raised the defence of reasonable chastisement and was acquitted by a majority verdict. The son appealed to the European Court of Human Rights which ruled that the UK had infringed its obligations under article 1 of the European Convention by failing to ensure the criminal law applied to the perpetrator of treatment which infringed article 3 of the Convention, which provides that no one shall be subjected to torture or to inhumane or degrading treatment (*A v UK* (1999)). The factors identified as being indicative of an unacceptable level of punishment included the age, health and size of the child, the nature and duration of the punishment and the lasting physical or psychological effect. The European Court did not therefore advocate a complete ban on corporal punishment of children, but thereafter any court considering a relevant case had to apply an interpretation of reasonable chastisement consonant with the jurisprudence of the European Court. Whilst on one view this was sufficient to ensure compliance with the Human Rights Act 1998 (*R v H (Assault of Child: Reasonable Chastisement)* (2001)), both international and national pressure for reform continued to grow (Smith 2004). During the passage of the Children Act 2004 through Parliament, cross-party attempts were made to introduce a new clause which would have abolished the defence of reasonable chastisement, and thus give children the same protection as adults from assault. However, the move was defeated in the House of Commons in November 2004 and s 8 of the Act, which was brought into force in January 2005, removes the defence of reasonable chastisement in relation to offences involving grievous and actual bodily harm under ss 18, 20 and 47 of the Offences Against the Children Act 1861 and the offence under s 1 of the Children and Young Persons Act 1933. As a result, the defence of reasonable chastisement can now only be relied upon in relation to a charge of common assault under s 39 of the Criminal Justice Act 1988. Legally any injury which is more than transient or trifling can be classified as actual bodily harm (*R v Donovan* (1934)), and therefore although a light smack which leaves no mark on a child is permissible, any physical punishment which leaves a bruise on the child or causes any other form of injury will, in theory, be subject to a criminal sanction.

Yet whilst it may still be acceptable to administer a gentle smack to a child as a form of discipline, any physical chastisement must necessarily be unacceptable in the case of infants who are too young to understand the difference between right and wrong and who thus are not susceptible to discipline. A child's age is therefore crucial to the question of reasonable chastisement and young infants should never be subjected to any form of physical chastisement. Whilst this may be accepted as a general proposition, research has found that three quarters of parents smack their babies in the first year of life, mostly as a result of irritation or anger (Smith 1995). Furthermore, even if a child is old enough to be disciplined, it is arguably never justifiable to administer any form of physical chastisement which is directed at the head or likely to result in injury to the head. Whilst this is only implicit in the legislation relating to England and Wales, legislation restricting the defence of reasonable chastisement in Scotland is explicit in this respect. Section 51(1) of the Criminal Justice (Scotland) Act 2003 requires a court when considering whether an assault on a child was justified in the exercise of parental right to consider a number of factors. However, s 51(3) of the Act goes on to provide that, if what was done included or consisted of a blow to the head, shaking or the use of an implement, the court *must* determine that the assault was not justified. The approach adopted by the Scottish legislation is arguably preferable to that adopted in England and Wales as it sends a clear message that NAHI to a child can never be justified as reasonable chastisement.

Acceptable parenting, reasonable chastisement and child protection

Child protection proceedings focus on the effect of the alleged abusive behaviour on the child rather than on the actions and culpability of the abuser. In order to satisfy the threshold criteria, it must be established that the harm, or likelihood of harm, is attributable to the care given to the child, or likely to be given to him if the order were not made, not being what it would be reasonable to expect a parent to give to him. Therefore, although the culpability of an individual perpetrator is not itself an issue, the standard of care given to the child will form an essential component of the court's consideration. Questions as to the acceptability of parental practices are therefore likely to be raised and judges must act as the 'judicial reasonable parent' (*J v C* (1969), p.831). Views as to what amount to acceptable parental practices are inevitably subject to change over the years and judges must take account of such changes in reaching their decisions. For example, 50 years ago corporal punishment of children with a cane or similar instrument was not unusual, yet today such conduct can be viewed as 'inhumane or degrading treatment or punishment' breaching article 3 of the European Convention on Human Rights and would no doubt also be viewed in an appropriate case as sufficient to satisfy the threshold criteria in s 31 on the footing that a reasonable parent would not resort to such measures (*CF v Secretary of State for the Home Department* (2004)).

More moderate corporal punishment may raise rather more difficult issues. Section 58 of the Children Act 2004, in addition to restricting the defence of reasonable chastisement in criminal proceedings, also provides that battery of a child causing ABH to the child cannot be justified in any civil proceedings on the ground that it constituted reasonable punishment. Although the threshold criteria in cases where it is alleged that a child has been abused require a finding that the child is suffering 'significant harm' –

which is not necessarily synonymous with a battery or ABH – in cases where a child has suffered actual bodily harm as a result of physical punishment there can be little doubt that the threshold criteria will be capable of being satisfied. Furthermore, considerations such as the age of the child and the infliction of any injury to the head will apply in child protection proceedings in the same way as they apply in criminal prosecutions (see above). In the future, any outright ban on corporal punishment that may be imposed will presumably impact on public and therefore judicial perceptions of acceptable parenting, but although the occasional light smack administered by a parent will not usually trigger child protection proceedings, cases involving young infants and NAHI will undoubtedly continue to be a cause for concern and will almost inevitably result in proceedings being taken.

Proving non-accidental head injury in legal proceedings: differing outcomes – inconsistent or inevitable?

The preceding discussion focuses on recent developments and considers the challenges faced in substantiating allegations of NAHI in legal proceedings. The discussion also highlights the fundamental distinctions between care proceedings and criminal prosecutions. Although the right to a fair trial contained in article 6 of the European Convention on Human Rights is applicable to both kinds of proceedings and applies at any stage of the litigation process (Re C (A Child) (Care Proceedings: Disclosure of Local Authority's Decision Making Process) (2002)), the impact of article 6 is very different in each case. In child protection proceedings the child's welfare is paramount and the court can consider an extensive range of evidence. Parents can be compelled to give evidence and are not entitled to refuse to answer questions on the grounds of self incrimination (Re Y (A Child) (Split Hearing: Evidence) (2003)). The co-operation of parents within the child protection system is encouraged by the creation of a 'sanctuary' in care proceedings within which they can admit to having abused the child without fear of adverse consequences in the criminal justice system (Cobley 2004). In contrast, in criminal prosecutions the central issues are the culpability of the defendant and the imposition of criminal sanctions following conviction. The presumption of innocence applies, the evidence on which the court can rely is restricted and the defendant cannot be compelled to give evidence, although in some circumstances adverse inferences can be drawn from his failure to give evidence (Criminal Justice and Public Order Act 1994, s 35). Such distinctions explain why differing findings of fact may result from the same allegation.

Yet the differing outcomes are frequently perceived as being inconsistent and the alleged abuser who is found in care proceedings to have abused a child but who is acquitted following a criminal trial is something of a conundrum to many. The simplest (and probably most generally proffered) explanation is the different standards of proof applicable in each of the proceedings, although, as shown above, there are a range of explanations which are considerably more complex, involving not only the different standards of proof, but the differing facts which must be proved and the range of evidence on which the fact finder can rely.

Arguably every case in which there are apparently conflicting findings of fact made in the family and the criminal courts can be explained on one or more of these grounds, yet on occasions the courts themselves have referred to the possibility of technically inconsistent findings being made. In *A Local Authority v S and W and T* (2004), a father had been acquitted of both the murder and manslaughter of his partner's child. In care proceedings relating to a surviving child of the family, it was found as a fact that the father had been responsible for the deceased child's death and that in so acting, he had had the requisite culpability to suffice for a conviction for manslaughter. Whilst this finding could have been justified solely on the different applicable standards of proof, Hedley J did not seek to do so but instead acknowledged that the finding may be technically inconsistent with the jury's acquittal of manslaughter. Arguably, such inconsistency would only arise if the finding had been made to the criminal standard of proof – a step which Hedley J was obviously not required to take and indeed, one which he did not expressly state he was taking, merely referring to being 'satisfied' that the defendant's actions were culpable. However, on the assumption that inconsistency may arise, he commented that he was sympathetic to a reluctance to expose the father to criminal punishment in the circumstances of the case, which he described as an 'uncharacteristic reaction, albeit a serious and culpable over-reaction, to a situation'.

Such reluctance to expose an abuser to criminal punishment or to reduce the severity of any sanction imposed has been referred to earlier in this chapter, but it is generally restricted to cases where an otherwise loving carer has lost control in an isolated incident and the decision-maker may feel a sense of 'there but for the grace of God go I'. In cases where the alleged abuser is seen as being truly culpable, the inability to secure a criminal conviction despite a finding of fact adverse to the abuser having been made in care proceedings can result in frustration and a perceived sense of injustice. In practice, professionals working within the criminal justice system will be fully aware of the difficulties encountered in securing criminal convictions in cases of alleged NAHI, although this knowledge will not prevent the inevitable feelings of frustration when certain defendants are acquitted and many child protection professionals may feel betrayed by a criminal justice system which allows those found in care proceedings to have injured a child to walk free. Yet, as we have shown in this chapter, such differing outcomes are not inconsistent, but are merely indicative of cases having reached different stages in the spectrum of proof. An understanding of the spectrum of proof and the specific challenges faced at each stage of the spectrum should therefore help alleviate any feelings of frustration and resentment between the professionals concerned and hopefully facilitate greater genuine multidisciplinary co-operation.

CHAPTER 5

Causation, Scientific Evidence and Shaken Baby Syndrome: An Example of a Medical Controversy

As we saw in Chapter 4, significant evidential problems can arise during court proceedings in alleged child abuse cases and medical expert evidence is frequently central to the outcome. In this chapter we explore the difficulties encountered by medical experts, the courts and the accused, focusing primarily on recent cases involving non-acidental head injury (NAHI). Child abuse may take many different forms ranging from minor cuts and bruises to life threatening injuries such as serious head trauma. For this reason it would be impossible and undesirable to examine all the issues arising from medical expert testimony in different types of non-accidental trauma. Consequently, we will limit ourselves to medical expert evidence in relation to NAHI and, more specifically, to cases of alleged shaken baby syndrome (SBS). In the current climate of evidence-based medicine (EBM), the question of how medical knowledge is utilised in cases of physical child abuse is of paramount importance for the effectiveness of the legal process and the protection of the victims. However, a number of problems are often evident in the use of experts. These may include conflicting opinion among witnesses, experts' lack of experience and preparation for engaging in an adversarial legal process, evidential pressure towards providing unequivocal expert opinion and the relationship between expert evidence/performance and outcomes. Increasingly, the demand for expert evidence has been met by a shortage of well-qualified specialists willing to offer their services to court, partly due to competing professional priorities and some hesitation about engaging in an adversarial legal system where professional credibility is likely to be challenged.

In the first part of the chapter we provide a backdrop to the subsequent discussion with an overview of the role of expert witnesses in legal proceedings and we then examine recent controversies surrounding the provision of expert evidence by clinicians. The implications for the status of medical expertise and professional legitimacy in the provision of expert opinion are discussed. The subsequent sections examine how medical expert evidence is used in the context of modern medical systems that increasingly expect practitioners to apply EBM. In particular, we explore the medical use of 'experiential' and 'scientific' knowledge in cases of child abuse, and evaluate the potential consequences of both types of knowledge on the provision of expert opinion. We question the assertion that experiential knowledge should be, or in fact can be, used separately in the provision of expert evidence. Finally, we explore the question of professional legitimacy in cases of physical non-accidental injury (NAI) in childhood. The chapter concludes with an examination of the nature of expertise by drawing on the work of Giddens (1991) to demonstrate how modern expert systems, including the medical and legal profession, are increasingly the objects of public scrutiny. We argue that although medicine seeks to protect its jurisdiction to an indeterminate knowledge base, through strategies such as 'occupational-closure', medical controversies have brought the status of medical expertise into question. The implications of this for the future role of medical expert witnesses in cases of child abuse are discussed.

The role of the expert witness in legal proceedings

Expert evidence has become an increasingly prominent feature of both civil and criminal litigation. As a general rule, witnesses may only give evidence of facts of which they have personal knowledge and are not allowed to give evidence as to their opinions. The rationale underlying the rule against evidence of opinion is that it is the function of the tribunal of fact (the judge in civil trials or the magistrates or jury in criminal trials) to draw inferences from the facts and to reach decisions about the application of the law to the facts. In general, the tribunal of fact has the competence to perform this task and so witnesses' opinions are unnecessary and superfluous and may even usurp the function of the fact finder. However, where an issue to be determined calls for a degree of skill and knowledge which is outside the experience of the tribunal of fact, expert witnesses may assist the tribunal in drawing the necessary inferences by giving evidence of their own opinion, based on their acquired expertise. During any proceedings, it is the responsibility of the judge to decide if there is a need for expert evidence and also to establish the competency of an expert witness. Expert witnesses are therefore uniquely placed to assist (and, on occasions, arguably to influence) the tribunal of fact. In theory, an expert witness's overriding duty is to the court and he or she is expected to give an objective, unbiased opinion on matters within his or her expertise. However, in practice, the provision of expert evidence to the courts raises several controversial issues.

In 1994 the Woolf Report reviewed the rules and procedures of the civil courts in England and Wales with a view to improving access to justice and reducing the cost of litigation (Woolf 1996). The report concluded that the cost of litigation was too high and devoted an entire chapter to the need for reforms in the use of expert evidence. Many of the recommendations were implemented in part 35 of the Civil Procedure Rules (CPR) which aims to control the volume, impartiality and quality of the evidence of experts who are instructed to give or prepare evidence for civil court proceedings. However, the emphasis placed by the Woolf Report and the CPR on 'neutral' expert opinion arguably conflicts with the adversarial nature of the legal system, which relies upon making a judgement about the evidence from two opposing positions. To this end, more complex cases, which require different arguments to be heard in order to resolve a problem, might find it more difficult to adhere to 'neutrality' in the provision of expert opinion (Friston 1999). The control of expert evidence in criminal proceedings is not as tightly regulated, although, as we discuss in Chapter 6, efforts are now being made to align the position in civil and criminal courts. However, in practice, in both civil and criminal proceedings, there remains a commonly held perception that expert witnesses are effectively 'hired guns'. In 2002, a survey of 133 expert witnesses found that 58 per cent did not think that lawyers encouraged their expert to be a 'truly independent witness' and 53 per cent of respondents said that there were firms of solicitors with whom they would never work again (although the reasons for this were not explored) (House of Commons 2005a, para 147).

Child abuse and the expert witness

Cases involving disputed allegations of child abuse provide fertile ground for the admission of evidence from a wide range of experts. The issues on which expert evidence may be required will depend on the nature of the proceedings and the facts of the individual case. Each issue tends to raise its own specific challenges, both for the experts themselves in presenting their evidence and for the courts in interpreting the evidence presented. For example, in child protection proceedings, experts may be called upon to assist the court in predicting any risk to child in the future and, as Brophy and Bates (1999) point out, the prognostic requirement as a predictive exercise in assessing future risk to a child is a new development in the law and one which requires specialist expertise. Research indicates that there is considerable disagreement among clinical experts (mainly psychiatrists) in child abuse cases regarding what constitutes child abuse and future risk (Brophy and Bates 1999). It is unclear whether these differences arise from clinicians' over-dependence on their clinical experience rather than on existing scientific evidence (Jones 1994).

Furthermore, criticisms have been made of the way in which expert evidence is presented to the court in cases of child abuse. One study found that diverse assessment procedures, often stemming from communication problems between experts in child abuse, led to the inability of courts to make independent assessments of the evidence presented (Gumpert and Lindblad 2001). Other investigations have pointed to discrepancies between psychologists' assessments in child sexual abuse situations, where they emphasised different aspects of a case in reaching their conclusions (Gumpert and Lindblad 1999). Borum and Grisso (1996) found in a study of criminal forensic reports that many experts failed to address legally relevant issues and established conclusions without supporting data or adequate reasoning. Others concluded, in relation to child sexual abuse, that evidential questions were poorly formulated and courts inadequately defined the expert role, leading to limited scrutiny and analysis of evidence (Allen and Miller 1995; Shuman *et al.* 1998). In civil cases the reform measures implemented following the Woolf Report, including the use of a single expert wherever the case concerns a substantially established area of knowledge, a co-operative approach between opposing experts, the disclosure of instructions on which the expert has acted, private meetings between experts and training for experts, have addressed many of the practical problems encountered in the presentation of expert evidence. We consider further proposals for reform of the provision of expert evidence to the courts in Chapter 6. It is the issue of causation and the medical controversy surrounding SBS that forms the basis of this chapter and it is to this topic that we now turn our attention.

Medical controversies and the role of expert evidence

Causation in the research cohort

As we discussed in Chapter 4, establishing the causation of any injuries sustained by a child will be a crucial element of proving abuse in both criminal prosecutions and child protection proceedings. A review of the medical literature undertaken before our research was carried out indicated that dispute as to the cause of conditions which may be indicative of abuse, such as subdural haemorrhage (SDH) and retinal haemorrhage (RH), would be the greatest obstacle to proving NAHI. Yet the cases in the research cohort revealed surprisingly little conflict of medical opinion on the issue of causation (Cobley *et al.* 2003; Cobley and Sanders 2003). Case records were examined and data extracted from reports and statements written by clinicians who either had direct contact with the child during admission to hospital, or who were invited to provide an expert opinion. The opinions of these clinicians were grouped according to the degree to which they believed the child had suffered NAHI, where one represented definite NAHI and seven represented definitely not NAHI. A maximum of five medical opinions were provided in any one case, although two or three opinions were provided in most cases. The majority of clinicians were of the opinion that the child's injuries had definitely, probably or possibly been caused non-accidentally.

Table 5.1: Medical opinion as to causation

	Number of opinions obtained	Mean
Medical opinion 1	53	2.13
Medical opinion 2	41	2.49
Medical opinion 3	27	2.22
Medical opinion 4	9	2.00
Medical opinion 5	2	1.50

An expressed conflict of medical opinion was noted in only ten cases in the study cohort. In seven of these ten cases, no arrest was made. In the other three cases, although both carers were arrested in each case, the suspects were released without charge in two of the cases. The father in the remaining case subsequently pleaded guilty to an offence of inflicting grievous bodily harm on the child and was sentenced to 12 months' imprisonment. Causation was contested at trial in only one case. A father charged with manslaughter denied causing the injury and suggested that the SDH could have been caused by wheeling the baby's pram along a bumpy path or alternatively, that it could have been caused by the victim's three-year-old sibling. Both explanations were rejected and the defendant was convicted. However, it appears from the court file that no medical evidence was called by the defence and so no direct conflict between experts arose in court.

Despite the surprisingly general consensus of opinion on causation found in the research cohort, the scientific evidence surrounding causation in cases of alleged SBS has become the focus of recent debate, and the ability of medical science to distinguish between accidental and non-accidental causes of the injuries has become contested in the light of scientific developments during the early years of the twenty-first century.

Controversy over the mechanism of injury in shaken baby syndrome: pathology versus injury

Research into the causes of infant deaths is thin on the ground, and experts frequently disagree about the causes, nature and circumstances of the injuries incurred. Causation in cases of alleged SBS has become particularly problematic to ascertain in light of new research that has recently been conducted by a group of researchers led by Dr Jennian Geddes (Geddes *et al.* 2001). As we have seen, prior to this research, SBS was a term applied to certain types of inflicted head trauma that seemed to explain the constellation of intracranial injuries exhibiting limited or no external signs of abuse, such as skull fractures. A general consensus existed among most paediatricians that there was a high probability of abuse in those cases where a young child presented with three physical symptoms that were considered to be signature marks of SBS, commonly referred to as the triad of injuries. However, following the research by Geddes, this hypothesis has been called into question.

Implicit in the term SBS rests the obvious assumption that the cause is non-accidental. For this reason, the onus of responsibility for child protection agencies such as the police and accident and emergency (A&E) departments has been simply to identify the triad of injuries as the classic signs of SBS. However, the research conducted by Geddes *et al.* (2001) casts doubt over the proposition that the triad observed in many cases of head trauma necessarily indicates a non-accidental cause. In fact, the findings (or their interpretation) were so striking that they seemed to call into question the actual existence of SBS. It is hardly surprising that the shockwaves resulting from this research would have far reaching implications for future court cases involving alleged SBS, and equally significantly for the nature of medical expert evidence. Geddes *et al.*'s (2001) study found that many cases of head trauma in children resulting in SDH and RH might have a physiological cause rather than a traumatic one. This belief is based on the finding that among the 53 child cases of fatal head injury that were studied, the resultant encephalopathy in infants was caused by hypoxic brain damage. Significantly, the study revealed no evidence of ruptured cells on the surface of the brain causing bleeding (diffuse traumatic axonal injury) usually caused by 'shaking' forces that often lead to the shearing of tissue on the surface of the brain. This finding suggested that the cause of death and the bleeding on the brain was caused by breathing difficulties (apnoea) leading to a restriction of oxygen to the brain, causing it to swell and subsequently to rupture blood vessels in the brain and eyes. Geddes *et al.* (2001) in turn proposed their own theory, dubbed the 'unified hypothesis', which proposed that all three elements of the triad could have a single cause and that cause *was not* necessarily traumatic. The single cause in this scenario, it was suggested, could be due to a lack of oxygen supply to the brain.

To add to this body of evidence relating to the potential causes of traumatic head injury, other researchers have investigated the issue of the degree of force that might be necessary to inflict head trauma that results in a similar pattern of intracranial injuries. Plunkett (2001), for instance, found that low-level falls in infants could potentially cause SDH and RH and lead to fatalities. Also, a biomechanical analysis found that fatality was possible during low-level falls, casting some doubt over the issue of whether an inflicted shaking injury is necessary *at all* to bring about the triad of injuries (Ommaya 2002). The hypothesis that 'external' trauma does not necessarily cause SBS has encouraged others to propose their own hypotheses, based on internal bodily mechanisms such as the association between bacterial toxins and the pathological changes produced by the triad of intracranial bleeding: 'The involvement of toxin signalling in some supposed "shaken baby" cases remains a tantalising prospect because toxin signalling is now well established as a major factor in the pathophysiological changes found in the victims of sudden infant death syndrome' (Kalokerinos 2005, p.22).

As we will show later, the emergence of new scientific hypotheses that seem to challenge existing ideas also creates opportunities for scientists and clinicians to make claims that support or challenge such new ideas. Giddens (1991) writes that the process of 'appropriation' of jurisdiction by one group often creates opportunities for other groups to develop their own ideas. Those who oppose the non-accidental explanation in cases of head injury often refer to other mechanisms or causes that originate within the body, and are therefore rejecting explanations that suggest an external cause. For instance, NAHI in children has often been attributed to congenital problems, rare birth defects or blood disorders. In support of this perspective, Geddes and Whitwell (2004) proclaim that their neuropathological study of fatal cases of infant head injury had led them to believe that: 'intracranial bleeding in NAI may be a secondary phenomenon resulting from *deranged infant physiology*, rather than a direct result of trauma' (our emphasis, p.87). What is being suggested here is that bleeding within the brain is often caused by physiological susceptibility or weaknesses that predispose certain infants to this type of injury, rather than from inflicted trauma. Consequently, the origin of the head trauma becomes located within the human body rather than in any external cause. Geddes and Whitwell (2004) have in essence placed SBS in a wider context of potential, predominantly physiological, causes whilst attributing only limited importance to external factors for the shaken baby hypothesis. The emergence of the Geddes research and subsequent events, which we discuss in detail in Chapter 6, emphasise the uncertainty of clinical evidence in this area of medicine.

De-contextualisation of non-accidental head injury

Is it possible that a greater focus on physiological causes will lead paediatricians and A&E physicians to overlook vital signs that might indicate a possible NAI? Geddes *et al.* (2001; Geddes and Whitwell 2004) seem to suggest that abusive head trauma only affects a minority of children and should only be considered in clinical assessment as one possibility among others. This proposition raises the question of how far clinicians will be encouraged to look for a clinical rather than a non-accidental cause in children presenting to A&E. As we discussed in Chapter 3, studies have shown that to assign limited importance to social and epidemiological factors in the identification of head trauma would be to omit a vital body of evidence that was likely to place children at risk (Sidebotham and Pearce 1997). Research shows that clinical and nursing staff, particularly in A&E, often fail to identify suspicious cases of head injury due to a lack of training and because of the tendency to search for a clinical cause (Haeringen *et al.* 1998; Jenny *et al.* 1999; Sundell 1997). If researchers are unwilling to accept the possibility of NAHI in young children, through a greater desire to identify and exclude possible clinical causes, the implications for court proceedings are likely to be significant. For example, as we saw in Chapter 4, in the absence of a confession by the perpetrator it is not possible to secure a criminal conviction if a medical cause for the injuries or death has not been excluded, even in cases where the social evidence is suggestive of abuse.

Bringing the 'social' back in

Research has also shown that serious head trauma in young children is rarely an isolated event, with many cases revealing signs of having sustained head injury or other types of physical injury on previous occasions (Sanders et al. 2003). During our research we found that 44 of 54 children suspected of sustaining NAHI presented with co-existing injuries such as bone fractures and bruising. We also found that the vast majority of the children in our case series came from deprived social backgrounds, although this does not necessarily indicate that NAHI is most likely to occur in families from lower socio-economic groups, because such cases may have been more likely to be referred to social services and police in the first place than those from higher socio-economic groups. If physiological factors explain many cases of NAHI, as suggested by Geddes and colleagues, it could therefore be assumed that such cases should be distributed relatively randomly in the population (geographically and based on socio-economic grouping). However, we know that such cases do not occur randomly, and in fact their incidence has a strong social gradient. As we discussed in Chapter 3, studies have shown that socio-economic and social factors are related to child abuse (Kotch et al. 1995; Whitehead and Drever 1999). Although epidemiological and sociological evidence can never offer conclusive proof that a child has been abused in any given case, it can provide a social and cultural profile of children who are most at risk. Should such evidence be ignored due to its low specificity for identifying NAI? Hobbs et al. (2005) used the Townsend Deprivation Score to conclude that NAHI occurred most frequently in the most deprived social classes, although they stated that reporting bias could have played a role in which children were referred to child protection agencies.

Geddes et al. (2001) suggest that a previous history of abuse should not interfere with the process of identifying the cause of the clinical signs. This proposition seeks to identify the causes of the clinical 'signs' or 'symptoms' by replacing a clinical focus on the mechanism of 'injury'. 'Injury' with its social connotations becomes reduced to an examination of the causes of the clinical 'features', where the assumption is no longer based on the belief that the child has sustained an externally inflicted injury. Indeed Geddes and Whitwell

122 / NON-ACCIDENTAL HEAD INJURY IN YOUNG CHILDREN

(2004) raise several points to distinguish further between the social/external and the physiological/internal causes of intracranial pathology. Although they acknowledge that fatal head trauma frequently results in the triad of injuries, they raise a number of objections to the assumption that only external causes explain this pattern of intracranial pathology. The points raised include the following:

- Extreme force can produce the triad of injuries consistent with SBS, although the level of force required to rupture bridging veins and cause subdural bleeding is unknown.

- The proposition that violence is the only cause of such injuries is wrong.

- Studies have been unable to distinguish between 'traumatic rupture' of the blood vessels on the brain and 'abnormal vascular' permeability (a physiological weakness of the blood vessel).

- In the immature brain, intracranial bleeding can be caused by hypoxia.

- Increased arterial pressure due to, for instance, blood pressure surges could also lead to SDH.

- In children with hypoxic brain swelling, venous leakage (in the subdural space) is greatly increased.

- Finally, in a genetically susceptible child any factor that triggers an episode of apnoea sufficient to cause severe hypoxic brain damage may precipitate subdural and retinal bleeding.

As can be seen, the focus here is predominantly on physiological aetiology despite the finding by some studies that SDH, RH and encephalopathy in infants under two years of age is most commonly found to be due to *trauma*, accidental or non-accidental (rather than from a 'natural' or a physiological abnormality) (Jayawant *et al.* 1998). In response to Geddes and colleagues, Kemp *et al.* (2003) argue that most SDHs in infancy occur as a result of NAHI when the infant has been shaken. They also argue that intracranial damage in infants is not only a radiological, neuropathological or clinical problem but also a socio-legal issue, suggesting that the focus in any clinical investigation should be on possible external causes of head trauma. To support these conclusions, a study by Hobbs *et al.* (2005) also concluded that trauma was the commonest cause of SDH. They found that out of 186 infants studied, 141 (75%) suffered trauma either accidentally or non-accidentally. The diagnosis of SDH was assisted by the presence of bruising and fractures without adequate history in 85 per cent of cases. It was concluded that bruises and fractures are rare in infants under the age of 12 months due to poor infant mobility. Reece expresses a need for researchers and medical practitioners to pool clinical, social and epidemiological evidence in order to address the issue of causality:

> Child abuse is an enormous social, medical, and mental health problem and its evaluation and treatment have far reaching implications for children, families and society. To provide optimal diagnosis and treatment, careful objective research, intellectual honesty are needed and must prevail over entrenchment of ideological schools of thought and 'winning' in court. Unfortunately there remains considerable difficulty for some doctors to accept that children are abused. We must locate cases using all the information available, including clinical experience and the synthesis of the best literature on the subject. (2004, p.1317)

This statement clearly suggests that researchers need to display greater scientific objectivity by refraining from making personal assumptions about the origin of intracranial bleeding that reflect their specific ideology. Also, Reece argues for a need not to divorce clinical experience from any assessment involving suspected NAHI. It is just this type of separation of *experience* from clinical *facts* that Geddes and colleagues have advocated with their focus upon internal mechanisms for ascertaining the causes of head trauma. The scientific reductionism advocated by Geddes and colleagues essentially removes clinical experience from the research process because experiential knowledge is susceptible to bias, and consequently is scientifically unreliable.

Others, however, put forward the opposite view with regard to experiential knowledge. Barton proclaims that 'identifying the best evidence for any question requires detailed appraisal, relevance, allocation, concealment...' (2000, p.256). From this perspective, scientific evidence does not stand alone; it has to be appraised particularly in relation to the individual experience of the clinician, but also in relation to other existing evidence. This view supports Sackett *et al.*'s (1997) 'hierarchy of evidence', which calls for research findings to be appraised critically in view of the clinician's experience. Indeed, the emergence of EBM is partly responsible for the greater importance placed on randomised controlled clinical trials, removing the potential for bias in research. Sackett *et al.*'s hierarchy of evidence also plays a significant role in its influence over what is considered to be valid evidence. According to Sackett *et al.* (1997) the most reliable type of scientific evidence is that which is based on randomised clinical trials. Other types of evidence are considered to be at the bottom of or further down the hierarchy. Despite this, Sackett and colleagues claim that all research should aspire to the randomised controlled trial ideal. The problem emerges, however, that certain subject areas, and head trauma in children is one such area, cannot be researched using randomised controlled methods. In such cases, it is argued, the best available scientific evidence should be utilised through a process of critical appraisal. As Barton argues:

> A similar debate took place centuries ago in English law. The legal 'best evidence rule' initially created a rigid hierarchy of evidence (that original written documents took precedence over oral evidence). It was replaced by the flexible principle that the weight given to each bit of evidence should be determined by a detailed appraisal of the characteristics of that evidence. (2000, p.256)

In contemporary cases of suspected NAHI in children the evidence base does not conform to Sackett's hierarchy because no randomised studies have been conducted, or could be conducted for that matter, on ethical principles. Instead, a variety of studies have attempted to address the problem of causation, including population case series, biomechanical as well as neuropathological investigations, all from different perspectives. However, most, if not all, of these investigations would fall short of Sackett's definition of 'high quality' scientific evidence. The problem that this proposition raises is that different clinicians will have different types and levels of experiential knowledge. For instance, a community paediatrician will be highly experienced in identifying suspected cases of child abuse not only from his or her clinical knowledge but also from interactions with patients and relatives. These clinicians commonly have extensive experience of attending case conferences in child abuse cases, interviewing relatives of patients and possess a detailed cumulative knowledge of the social, cultural and economic influences on NAI in children. As a result, they are likely to offer experiential knowledge that is distinctly different from that offered by a neuropathologist or a radiologist, who may have a more specialised understanding of paediatric pathology or knowledge of a specialist branch of child health, but a much more limited grasp of associated, epidemiological and sociological factors. Consequently, the scientific evidence that is appraised by a community paediatrician will differ from that appraised by a neuropathologist.

Geddes and Whitwell (2004) are critical of past research conducted on the causes of head trauma. They claim that few neuropathological studies have been conducted on infant head injury, 'merely a few series looking at specific aspects, such as tissue tears, mechanisms of injury...' (p. 83). However, their conclusion that past studies are limited because they fail to examine the neuropathological factors in disease causation seems overly critical, especially as it is sometimes difficult to see how studies that offer a narrow focus on the internal pathology of head trauma can adequately comment on the likely external causes of injury. It is precisely the sorts of studies that Geddes and colleagues criticise that often lead to an improved understanding of the external mechanisms of injury. Moreover, Geddes and Plunkett (2004a) argue that the lack of certainty resulting from research studies conducted on head trauma in infants even casts doubt on the existence of SBS. They go further to suggest that 'good quality science' is needed to identify more clearly the causes of such head injuries, and suggest that: 'a natural desire to protect children should not lead anyone to proffer opinions unsupported by good quality science' (p.720). However, Geddes et al.'s (2001) neuropathological study on a sample of 53 fatal cases of head trauma also falls short of Sackett's gold standard, particularly as it did not use control groups, double-blind methods, adopt an experimental design or conduct a meta-analysis or a systematic review of the literature.

Geddes and colleagues also seem to be proposing, with their tight focus on physiological causes, that the only type of valid evidence is predominantly clinical, which consequently removes any external, sociological and psychological dimension from medical reasoning. Moreover, their focus on physiology consequently seems to presume that a focus on the 'internal mechanics' of the human body will further remove medical uncertainty. However, others disagree with this view, which implies that one set of principles can on their own account for and explain the complexity inherent in certain clinical problems. Kuhlmann argues the following, in relation to EBM and the scientific community's eagerness to deny subjectivity and uncertainty in clinical judgement: 'Although it (EBM) comes out on top as the new paradigm and downplays its tensions with discretionary, context-based, clinical decision-making, it does not overcome medical and biomedical uncertainty' (2004, p.6). She calls for the need to utilise a variety of methodologies, and to dismantle the artificial separation of science and experience: 'Hereby, science and practice are placed in a hierarchical order that devalues embodied knowledge of patients as well as providers, and clinical experience of clinicians.' Similarly, Blanc and Burau criticise the assumption made by advocates of EBM that science is objectively neutral and value free:

> From the perspective of doctors, evidence-based medicine is ambiv-alent. Evidence-based medicine promises to strengthen the scientific nature of medicine by reducing unwarranted variation in diagnostic and therapeutic practice. At the same time, guidelines may encourage a standardised approach to practice and constrain the leeway for professional judgement (2004, p.136).

Recent research that has focused on the internal mechanics of head trauma in children is in some ways reducing clinical judgement to a more narrow set of biomedical principles that exclude a broader set of theoretical perspec-tives and hypotheses. Kuhlmann reiterates this point in relation to scientific practice more generally:

> There is an urgent need for transparency in decision-making and for a reduction of unintended variation, but there is no need for a 'one-size-fits-all' standard and unique truth of evidence. The reductionist logics and tools of the randomised, double-blind, pla-cebo-controlled trial are not *the* scientific method, but only one of many. (2004, pp.6–7).

Quoting Best and Glik (2003), Kuhlmann claims that 'a new partnership perspective that brings together the best of both reductionistic and holistic paradigms' is required' (p.250).

'Science' as legitimation in shaken baby syndrome

Medicine's success in presenting itself as a profession closely aligned with science has helped to secure its legitimacy and its high professional status. The status accorded to different sub-specialist areas of medicine varies widely, however. For instance, highly specialised branches of medicine such as cardiology often have a high professional status, whereas generalist fields of medicine, such as general practice or geriatrics, tend to command a lower professional standing. Status stratification is also influenced by the extent to which different medical professionals 'use' science in their work and the success with which their particular area of medical practice is presented as being 'scientific'. Thus, to conceive of medicine as a well integrated and cohesive system of medical practice and scientific knowledge is strictly flawed, as such a perspective fails to account for the differences in status, autonomy and public trust that different branches of medicine command. As we shall see, Fleck (1935) recognised the existence of variation in 'thought styles' within any single scientific community, including medicine. He showed how some medical specialities adopted a more pervasive scientific rhetoric than other groups in order to make knowledge claims to particular fields of practice.

Abbott (1988) has questioned the utility of treating the medical profession as a cohesive entity, and preferred to conceptualise modern medicine as comprising a 'system' of professions, made up of interdependent groups of professionals, and occupations within a larger profession, each competing to secure its jurisdiction. Furthermore, he argues that the modern medical profession has come to rely upon science as a means of legitimation. For instance, Foley and Faircloth (2003) found that in order to establish themselves as equal to doctors, the midwives in their study often used the rhetoric of science to show that they also possessed a specialist knowledge base. Adoption of the 'scientific' rhetoric has been utilised in the ensuing debate surrounding the causes of intracranial bleeding in infants. Proponents and critics of the shaken baby hypothesis have selectively used scientific research evidence and adopted the scientific rhetoric to strengthen their respective cause, although in distinctly different ways. We will now outline some of these rhetorical uses of science as a means of securing professional legitimacy.

Gieryn (1983) proclaimed that professional boundaries are inherently contradictory. In our case we refer to the professional boundaries between two groups of paediatricians: those who support and those who refute the shaken baby hypothesis. Paediatricians are defined as professionals with a specialist interest in child health, which include community or general paediatricians. Others also can have a specialist interest in child health, including neuropathologists, pathologists, neurosurgeons and radiologists. It is not difficult to see how clinicians from such different clinical backgrounds might disagree on specified areas of uncertainty in medicine. In Gieryn's (1983) view the contradiction essentially relates to the idea that professionals not only have a duty to uphold the scientific basis of their work, but also to satisfy their professional interests, which often involves protecting their specific area of professional work or jurisdiction. It is therefore evident that the case of SBS has become a focus for debate in the clinical domain of child health. So how have the participants in the debate used the scientific rhetoric to further their respective positions on the issue?

Opponents of the shaken baby hypothesis have frequently referred to studies or literature reviews that seem to refute the existence of the syndrome. For instance, Geddes and Plunkett (2004a) refer to the literature review conducted by Donohoe (2003) and Lantz *et al.* (2004):

> The recent literature contains a number of publications that *disprove* traditional expert opinion in the field [re: existence of SBS]. A study of independently witnessed low-level falls showed that such falls may prove fatal, causing both subdural and retinal bleeding. A biomechanical analysis *validates* that serious injury or death from a low level fall is possible and *casts doubt* on the idea that shaking can directly cause retinal or subdural haemorrhages. (p.719, our emphasis)

This quotation is used to argue, with reference to two recent studies of low-level falls, that the evidence supporting the existence of SBS is inadequate. Uses of terms such as 'disprove', 'validates' and 'casts doubt' present previous research as essentially flawed, even though Geddes and Plunkett refer to only two studies quoted in the review to argue their case. One is a literature review, which does not in itself represent original empirical research, whilst the other is a biomechanical study based on non-human subjects, which raises doubt about how the evidence can subsequently be applied to human infants. Geddes and Plunkett (2004a) continue to assert their criticism of the 'unscientific' nature of past research in relation to the literature review conducted by Lantz *et al.* (2004):

> Lantz et al were able to find only two *flawed* case controlled studies, much of the published work displaying an absence of precise and reproducible case definition, and interpretations or conclusions that overstep the data...the evidence for shaken baby syndrome appears analogous to an inverted pyramid, with a very small database (most of it *poor quality* original research, *retrospective* in nature, and without *appropriate control groups*. (p.719, our emphasis)

Again, it is argued that the evidence supporting the shaken baby hypothesis is either of poor quality, flawed or retrospective. The authors, however, fail to show specifically which aspects of the hypothesis are flawed. Even though they acknowledge the difficulty of conducting prospective, randomised controlled trials on infants, they nevertheless use the 'flawed research' argument to criticise the evidence-base in this field. The same 'flawed research' argument could equally be applied to the studies that they quote in *support* of their own hypothesis (e.g. that intracranial bleeding is often not due to abuse). Advocates of the shaken baby hypothesis, on the other hand, also rely on science to argue their case. For instance, in the opening sentence of a letter to the editor of the British Medical Journal criticising Geddes and Plunkett's assertion that research on SBS is flawed, Reece states:

> In challenging the diagnosis of shaken baby syndrome in their recent editorial Geddes and Plunkett make a number of serious errors in interpreting the research on this issue, and they display a worrisome and persistent bias against the diagnosis of child abuse in general. (2004, p.1316)

Whilst challenging their scientific interpretation of the evidence, Reece goes further to say that those who solely advocate a neuropathological cause in intracranial bleeding in infants, levelling his point at Geddes and Plunkett (2004a), invariably fail to account for previous, milder (and therefore undetected) episodes of SDH. In his statement, Reece argues that Geddes and Plunkett's focus on physiological causes is essentially reductionistic and analyses cases of head trauma as 'isolated' events. He continues with reference to Geddes and Plunkett's omission of vital scientific evidence in their hypotheses: 'This is in conflict with the research of Alexander et al, Ewing-Cobbs et al, Kemp et al, and Jenny et al, who found that 30–40% of newly diagnosed shaken baby cases had medical evidence of previously undiagnosed head injury' (p.1316). Geddes and Plunkett (2004b) respond to the shortcomings of one of the studies that Reece cites, by referring again to the scientific limitations inherent in research conducted in the past: 'We would urge them to look again, for example, at the paper they cite by Alexander et al, where they will find all the above shortcomings' (p.1317). Reece (2004), however, continues by identifying the shortcomings of research that has attempted to challenge the shaken baby hypothesis, widely cited by Geddes and colleagues. Reece criticises Geddes and Plunkett's (2004a) assertion that doctors should not assume that the presence of RH are indicative of NAI. However, he claims that they fail to underscore the findings of a number of studies which have shown that RH are significantly more *frequent* in abusive cases than in accidental cases:

One study analysed these obviously non-inflicted injuries and compared them with abusive head injuries in children under 6 years of age. Severe retinal haemorrhages were seen in 5 of the 233 (2%) children in the non-inflicted group and in 18 of the 54 (33%) in the abusive group. (p.1316)

This observation seems to suggest that differences exist in the nature of the external trauma – a conclusion that is supported by Betchel *et al.* (2004) who conclude that RH in infants with abusive head trauma were far more extensive than those from non-accidental injuries. They proclaim that it is not the *presence* of RH that is significant, as Geddes and colleagues argue, but their *number, location* and *distribution* that will enable a clinician to distinguish between accident and abuse. In order to pursue their case, advocates of SBS have also asserted the need to examine the external as well as the internal causal mechanisms of intracranial bleeding in order not to simplify the complexity of the issue. The general stance has been to present intracranial bleeding in infants as more of a complex phenomenon than its opponents suggest, asserting the need to rely on scientific evidence from clinical studies and case histories, but also on social and legal evidence. Their 'moral' argument has been to suggest that a clinical hypothesis that offers a 'one-size-fits-all' solution based on aggregate data will serve to overlook the individual and highly specific nature of such cases. Kemp *et al.*'s (2003) point of departure is the belief that intracranial bleeding in infants is caused by external trauma (accidental or non-accidental), and as such they propose a highly 'contingent' theory:

> The factors associated with shaking are multiple and the forces elicited will vary according to the mechanism of injury, be it shaking or shaking impact, the strength and the intention of the perpetrator, the size and muscle tone of the baby, and where the baby is held... Decisions on forces and mechanisms of injury in this field are clearly complex... The current evidence base is insufficient to make any accurate comment about the degree of force that would be necessary to cause intracranial damage. It is important that multi-agency collaborative research to pool biomechanical, clinical, neuropathology, radiology, and socio-legal findings continues to build up this source. (p.475)

Kemp *et al.* advocate a more flexible approach to, and use of, evidence during the course of appraising cases of head trauma. They reject the proposition that only best quality research as evidenced by the use of case-controlled studies and randomised trials is acceptable, with the contention that a broad range of evidence, clinical as well as social is required, and should be utilised in the assessment of abusive head trauma. Kemp's (2002) statement asserts the importance that supporters of the shaken baby hypothesis attach to evidence that is not necessarily scientific but could be used during initial and subsequent clinical assessments:

> The Local Authority Child Protection Team must be involved early to undertake preliminary investigations and exclude any previous concerns of child abuse within the family unit. Early involvement of the police will identify relevant criminal records of the child's carers and ensure that any forensic investigation can be initiated as soon as possible. (p.99)

This position is equally reflected in the views of Wynne and Hobbs (1998):

> Diagnosis of child abuse is likened to completion of a jigsaw... The diagnosis of shaken baby syndrome is made on the *history*, examination (bruises, burns, retinal haemorrhages, and other eye injuries), and investigations. (p.815, our emphasis)

Kleinman (1998) makes a similar observation in relation to the complex and multi-factorial dynamics inherent in identifying child abuse, where there exists a tendency to oversimplify the issues. In response to an editorial which criticised the lack of clinical evidence supporting the shaken baby hypothesis, the following views were expressed:

> In court, be it criminal or family proceedings, conviction (or removal of a child from its carers) is never a consequence of the medical evidence alone. The statements of the suspect carers and their performance in the witness box weigh just as heavily with the judge and jury, if not more so, than medical evidence. (Green 1998, p.816)

The customary practice of experienced physicians is to view clinical and imaging findings suspicious of abuse in conjunction with all other imaging data, clinical findings and *historical* information (Kleinman 1998, p.815).

'Thought collectives' and 'thought styles' in the construction of medical knowledge

In 1935 Ludwick Fleck wrote a monograph entitled 'Genesis and Development of a Scientific Fact', in which he described the development of scientific knowledge as a process of interaction occurring between different 'thought collectives'. Thought collectives comprise an 'esoteric' centre made up of scientific experts and an 'exoteric' outer circle composed both of educated people and uneducated lay persons. Fleck believed that medical facts are established through a process of exchange and circulation of ideas between experts and the wider public. Implicit in Fleck's argument is the view that scientific knowledge cannot be separated from the historical timeframe and the cultural context in which it originates. Within the thought collective exists a 'thought style', which links the individual participants of a collective together, whilst simultaneously shaping and constraining the style of thought that is adopted. Fleck proposes that individuals within a thought collective who share a thought style are unable to think differently to the accepted mode of thought adopted by a particular thought collective. However, within a given thought style, a number of different, even seemingly competing, theories and ideas can coexist. In addition, whilst medicine could be perceived as comprising a number of clinical sub-specialities, the thought style that dominates medicine is at one and the same time specific to each sub-speciality. Consequently, it is entirely possible, within Fleck's model, for all clinicians to share the same or a similar thought style, whilst simultaneously advocating competing theories and propositions. Within medicine, different sub-specialities possess the thought style specific to their specialist discipline. Thus, general medicine will have a different thought style to obstetrics. However, this difference does not necessarily preclude communication and the exchange of ideas between professionals, although some have more in common with each other than others. In relation to NAHI, paediatricians and neuropathologists may exist as part of the same community of clinicians, or thought collective, although their specific thought styles will differ. This does not mean that they will not communicate with one another, but that their individual thought styles may under certain conditions lead to disagreement.

According to Fleck, therefore, scientific facts are intrinsically bound to a particular thought collective, and so any attempt to legitimate a particular approach (or scientific observation) as the correct one is inherently flawed. In the context of NAHI, Fleck would argue that to reduce the causes of intracranial bleeding either to internal, physiological factors, as suggested by Geddes and colleagues, or to external factors such as physical *trauma*, as argued by proponents of the shaken baby hypothesis, is misconceived. Both perspectives are tied to their specific thought styles and therefore to choose the hypothesis that lies 'closer to reality' would, according to Fleck, be meaningless. Thus far, Fleck's concept of thought style appears to be a fruitful way of conceptualising the exchange of scientific ideas between different groups within a thought collective. However, his view that scientists are bound by their specific thought style and cannot think beyond it is too rigid. Fleck suggests that a scientist's ability to observe and interpret facts is restricted by the specific sub-specialist field in which he or she has been educated. It does not extend to other fields of science:

> I knew an eminent surgeon, specialising in the abdominal cavity, who needed only just a few looks and a few touches of the abdomen to diagnose the clinical state of the appendix vermiformis almost infallibly, sometimes in cases when other medical men 'did not see anything'. The same specialist could never learn how to distinguish under a microscope mucus from the hyaline cast. (1935, p.60)

Fleck makes a perfectly reasonable distinction between the skills of a surgeon as requiring the employment of radically different thought processes to a microbiologist. Although their individual thought styles enabled them to see different aspects of the same reality, it is clear that their specific thought styles were so different that they were likely to reach different conclusions about the phenomena they observed. However, the thought styles of clinicians working in different specialist areas of child health are perhaps likely to share basic knowledge and principles relating to paediatric medicine, more so than the surgeon and microbiologist in the above example. Moreover, Fleck's conceptualisation of the thought style within a collective of medical specialists lacks 'permeability'. For instance, he does not recognise the possibility that some neuropathologists will support the shaken baby hypothesis, just as there will inevitably be paediatricians who refute it, and vice versa. Residence within a specific clinical speciality does not necessarily constrain a professional's 'thought style' in a way that is suggested. The development of scientific knowledge within medicine could also be viewed as a conflict between the pressure to ground clinical decisions on rationalistic, systematic and standardised evidence on the one hand and the ability of clinicians to utilise experiential knowledge in the decision-making process. Thus, the thought styles of a medical expert do not only reflect their own disciplinary background, but also the different and possibly competing modes of thought of individual experts. We will now examine this proposition to illustrate the tension that exists at the centre of the current debate about the causes of head trauma in alleged cases of SBS.

Science versus experience in non-accidental head injury

So far we have discussed the nature of scientific evidence in relation to NAHI, and how its construction is contingent upon the cultural and social context. We have argued that biological as well as methodological reductionism, as proposed by Sackett *et al.* (1997), does not necessarily lead closer to an objective 'truth' especially when the research evidence in NAHI in children strongly suggests that contingent (external) factors play a part in explaining the causes of such injuries. In this section we are not concerned with theoretical issues of scientific validity and reliability, but with the *practical* application of medical knowledge in cases of uncertainty.

For centuries medical practice has been characterised by an inert tension between using the most reliable, scientific evidence to guide clinical judgement and reaching decisions based on clinical experience, or experiential knowledge. It is argued that an uncritical adoption of the latest evidence in clinical decision-making de-contextualises medical judgement and overlooks the uncertain nature of medical knowledge and problem solving (Sackett *et al.* 1997). On the other hand, adopting experiential knowledge without reference to current research in a particular field of medicine is likely to result in decisions that are outdated or no longer accepted in medical practice. The solution that is proposed is to utilise both approaches. The recent cases of Sally Clark and Angela Cannings and subsequent events relating to expert witnesses (which we discuss in detail in Chapter 6) highlight an inherent contradiction in the expectation of the courts and the expert's desire to provide the best expert opinion based on his or her expertise. We noted at the beginning of this chapter that an expert witness's overriding duty is to the court and he or she is expected to give an objective, unbiased opinion on matters within his or her expertise. As the Attorney General (2004) noted, an expert is not there as a hired gun, as advocate for one cause or another, but to help the court reach a verdict. However, prosecution and defence teams in cases of suspected child abuse frequently select experts who they believe will offer them a favourable opinion. The issue of impartiality also raises the question about the definition of 'expertise', which includes some element of personal judgement, otherwise the need for experts would be unnecessary as research-based scientific evidence could easily be obtained without external professional input. Consequently, the question that arises is how much of a clinician's individual experience should be used in court proceedings? Moreover, the personal experience of individual clinicians can also contradict the research evidence, as it is based on a more biased appraisal of cases of suspected abuse. Scientific evidence, however, is more systematic and less relevant to individual cases, and does not take into account the unique context surrounding individual situations in a way that a clinician's experiential knowledge might.

The expert–lay divide

So far, we have discussed the construction of scientific facts and examined the issues that validate different sets of scientific principles and hypotheses, with particular reference to the social and cultural influences on knowledge construction. Furthermore, our analysis has concentrated on the exchange and circulation of ideas among medical experts residing in the 'esoteric' circle. In this section we will move towards an examination of the interactions occurring between different 'thought collectives' including medical experts, the wider public and the legal system.

First, we refer to Arksey's (1994) study of lay and expert participation in the social construction of repetitive strain injury (RSI) to illustrate this interaction between thought collectives. Arksey argues that orthopaedic surgeons and rheumatologists are both concerned with controlling the definition of RSI. The former seek to prove that the syndrome does not have a physiological basis and therefore can only be explained as a psychological response of the complainant, and the latter believe in the physical existence of RSI through the adoption of a holistic style of practice, facilitating recognition between localised pain and signs in the musculo-skeletal system. According to Fleck's conceptualisation, both groups of physicians uphold incommensurable thought styles, in a similar way to a microbiologist and a paediatrician, for example.

Arksey (1994) also shows that the way medical knowledge is shaped extends beyond the 'core set' of medical experts to include the public. She argues that the public have been instrumental in shaping the debate with the scientific community about the very existence of RSI, largely on an individual basis through raising awareness by discussing their illness with GPs, but also by forming relations with the media and support groups. In a similar way, knowledge about SBS has been constructed through interaction between the scientific community (medical experts), the public and the legal system. In this case the nature of scientific knowledge in SBS has been highly politicised and, as Fleck would argue, it is a reflection of the social and cultural climate of the day. Consequently, the interaction between medical knowledge and the public moderates the scientific acceptability of SBS, and as we shall show, this interaction frequently occurs within the legal system where the definition of SBS becomes a 'battleground' between the advocates and the critics of the syndrome.

Moral responsibility, rhetoric and the medical expert

Arksey's research on expert and lay discourses in RSI showed that clinicians used a highly politicised rhetoric in academic journals and the popular literature, and did not only rely on science to justify their acceptance or rejection of the condition. She shows how some doctors expressed a need to consider carefully the implications of the diagnosis for society as a whole, often raising concern about the potential for claimants to seek compensation from their employers. Others opposed RSI by comparing the public response to mass hysteria.

In the case of the shaken baby hypothesis, a similar debate has ensued between advocates and opponents of the theory. Both parties have utilised a rhetorical discourse with which to justify their position. Advocates of SBS proclaim a moral and social responsibility to protect infants from abuse, whilst its opponents have asserted the need to protect innocent people from wrongful conviction. Geddes and Plunkett (2004b) argue thus: 'When there is new evidence that challenges an established conviction, medicine has the responsibility to critically evaluate the data, and if verifiable, reflect that change. We must have no vested interest in yesterday's belief' (p.1317). According to the authors, clinicians have a responsibility to ensure that scientific evidence is used accurately and that medical knowledge is not misrepresented. They subsequently refer to the legal context, and how medical evidence has the potential for misrepresentation, arguing that the medical expert must have a moral responsibility to the patient, but also to ensure that justice is achieved. Geddes and Plunkett (2004a) refer to the assumption often made by clinicians that intracranial bleeding is predominantly the result of abuse:

> These beliefs are reinforced by an interpretation of the literature by medical experts, which may on occasion be instrumental in a carer being convicted or children being removed from their parents... If

the issues are much less certain than we have been taught to believe, then to admit uncertainty sometimes would be appropriate for experts. Doing so *may make prosecution more difficult*, but a natural desire to protect children should not lead anyone to proffer opinions unsupported by good quality science. (p.720, our emphasis)

There is a clear appeal to clinical responsibility for protecting the accused in the criminal courts, by admitting uncertainty if the science suggests that significant uncertainty exists. This example illustrates the implications of clinical opinion on the wider legal context in child abuse, but it also shows how clinical opinion might in turn be influenced by the legal implications of expert evidence. For instance, it is no coincidence that Geddes and Plunkett discuss the legal consequences of clinical uncertainty in proving the causes of head trauma in infants, certainly because this argument is used to strengthen their own case in favour of a neuropathological explanation. Similarly, proponents of the shaken baby hypothesis have also recognised the legal implications of research, especially that which challenges the existence of the theory. Kemp *et al.* (2003) for instance, claim:

These statements have had a significant impact on the criminal justice system, as a recent decision by the Court of Appeal indicates…[in which] the Court was referred to the research [of Geddes and colleagues] and concluded that [in one particular case] the less serious charge of manslaughter was the only safe verdict. (p.472)

A similar view is shared by a forensic pathologist, who refers to the legal implications of experts providing unsubstantiated beliefs on the causes of head trauma in infants: 'Child abuse in any form is always unacceptable. However, if errors in diagnosis, false accusations, and wrongful convictions result from untested and unverified beliefs, then we have done harm' (Lantz 2004, p.741).

Advocates of the shaken baby hypothesis have frequently referred to the public's 'moral' responsibility for protecting children at risk of abuse. Professor Sir Roy Meadow, for instance, was quoted as suggesting 'it is a national scandal that we accept a situation in which so many young children die of unknown causes. If one out of every thousand 21 year olds died suddenly and unexpectedly without an identifiable cause, there would be a national outcry' (White 1999, p.147). Similarly, Marcovitch (1999), a specialist in child health, offered an emotive response to the unwillingness of many doctors and the legal system to recognise child abuse:

> I still recall with anger the magistrate, in 1969, who closed his eyes as
> I described the burnt feet of a child who had been plunged into a hot
> bath; in his blindness he preferred to accept defence counsel's spuri-
> ous argument that the injuries were caused by tight shoes. (p. 950)

Marcovitch addresses the critics of the National Society for the Prevention
of Cruelty to Children (NSPCC)'s Full Stop campaign, which began with a
series of uncompromising television commercials, where the message was
that people hide from child abuse because facing up to it is too painful: 'I
hope that paediatricians especially, but all doctors generally, will line up
with the NSPCC and ignore those cynical commentators who have already
started sniping at the campaign from the safety of their Sunday broadsheet
columns' (p.950). Others have proclaimed that controversy benefits the
defence as the onus is on the prosecution to prove abuse (National Centre on
Shaken Baby Syndrome).

In the USA, the National Centre on Shaken Baby Syndrome, which
aims to prevent serious child abuse through prevention and educational
campaigns, provides a number of fact sheets on SBS aimed at educating the
public about the syndrome and preventing future child abuse. It criticises
the current system of child protection, particularly in relation to some of the
legal loopholes often exploited by the defence in legal cases. It also provides
a moral critique of the 'irresponsible' uses of medical 'expert' evidence in
court. It is suggested that defence counsel often exploit the clinical uncertainty surrounding the causes of SBS in order to introduce reasonable
doubt, which might be achieved by identifying alternative accidental or
physiological causes of abuse. Holmgren, a legal advisor to the National
Centre on Shaken Baby Syndrome, states: 'there is an incentive for those
defending against allegations of child abuse to throw up an expert on the
other side – to create controversy, whether one legitimately exists or not'
(Holmgren 1999). Accordingly, the defence might suggest that the medical
findings result from a disease process such as meningitis, alagille syndrome,
glutaric aciduria or adverse reactions from diphteria (DTP) vaccinations.
Experts acting for the defence may also suggest that cardiopulmonary resus-
citation (CPR) or childbirth could have caused RH, and a skull fracture
could be caused accidentally from a fall. Holmgren further states that the
defence's expert opinion need only suggest a possibility that the injuries
were not as a result of abuse, to create doubt. The suggestion that irresponsible expert testimony disadvantages the prosecution is illustrated by

Chadwick and Parrish (2000) who raise a number of issues which suggest that 'scientific' evidence is reconstructed within the legal arena, consequently becoming politicised rather than remaining 'objective' and value free. They contend that the uses of 'preliminary' research findings in court by defence counsel can lead to misrepresentation of evidence, especially if such findings are made public. It is claimed that an important form of irresponsible expert testimony is one that is described as the unique causal theory whereby the 'expert' connects a cause and an effect in a way which has never been described in peer reviewed medical literature. In short, the 'expert' invents the causal relationship for use in court in spite of the fact that it has no other existence. However, in an adversarial legal system where both sides choose medical experts precisely because they are most likely to offer a favourable view for their case, it is difficult to see how controversy in medical opinion will ever be avoided.

These claims present a picture of the legal system in which cases involving children who have allegedly been shaken are open to manipulation by, mainly, defence lawyers. The views of professionals who support the shaken baby hypothesis present their case as one that is wholly moral, in contrast to those opposing it, who seek to protect the interests of the accused or medical opinion which refutes the existence of SBS. Once the medical controversies surrounding SBS enter the public and legal domain, the 'science' of head trauma becomes redefined, and the use of 'discursive' strategies by both sides are common practice. The intention is to use medical opinion as a tool for presenting a specific moral argument. This type of moral discourse becomes even more pervasive when the public gain access to such controversies through the media. It is to this final issue that we will now turn.

Medical controversies and the mediation of expertise: the legal context

A number of medical experts have recently been criticised by judges for misrepresenting the evidence or misleading the court through the provision of 'erroneous' opinion. However, there is an inherent contradiction between the court's expectation that the expert offers certainty and the experiential knowledge of the expert witness, whose opinion is based on both technical knowledge *and* experience. The contradiction resides in the legal system's assumption that the two characteristics, knowledge and experience, are separable. In practice, they seldom are. Fleck's (1935) idea of incommensurate thought styles reflects the tension between medical science and the legal system, where the latter demands certainty whilst the former can rarely provide it in controversial cases such as in SBS. Consequently, the legal system can influence the legitimacy or credibility that is attributed to medical evidence, especially in cases where existing knowledge is contested. Media coverage of child abuse cases has highlighted the way judges have criticised experts for misrepresenting the evidence, often in relation to the mechanics of the injury. Thus, the legal system has become an important forum for the mediation of clinical uncertainty. As we noted at the beginning of this chapter, there is a commonly held perception that expert witnesses are effectively 'hired guns' which suggests that the legal system is inherently contradictory because it expects impartiality from the expert, whilst parties to proceedings perceive the utility of the expert in terms of the 'ammunition' he or she can provide in support of their case. However, it has also been argued that the adversarial system is essential because it enables the evidence to be tested by both sides (Norfolk 1997). It is to this end that discrepancies are identified in the arguments of medical experts representing the defence and prosecution. According to this view, the medical evidence is played out in court where opposing positions are scrutinised, and where certain types of medical opinion are accepted or refuted. This pattern is evident in the judgement of the Court of Appeal in the case of *R v Harris and others* (2005), the facts of which we discuss in detail in Chapter 6. As we shall see, the research by Geddes and colleagues was instrumental in the outcome of two of the appellants who had their convictions quashed, but more significantly the judgement demonstrates the adjudication of scientific evidence between the two opposing positions and the legal system.

In its judgement, the Court of Appeal rejected the notion that the triad of intracranial injuries by themselves was necessarily indicative of abuse, although it was acknowledged that the triad was a 'strong pointer to NAHI on its own' (para 70). Having heard the evidence, the Court did not think it possible to find that the triad must 'automatically and necessarily lead to a diagnosis of NAHI', but emphasised that all the circumstances, including the clinical picture, had to be taken into account. In fact, as we discussed in Chapter 3 the term 'diagnosis' has frequently been used in media reports and by clinicians when referring to the triad of injuries which is thought to indicate shaking injuries in children. Thus, reference to SBS as a diagnosis rather than a 'syndrome' could be viewed as a 'legitimacy' claim utilised by many clinicians, where the clinical reality of the intracranial injuries is perceived to be synonymous with abuse.

On the other side of the coin, the 'unified hypothesis', advocated by Geddes and colleagues, which suggests that the triad of injuries can be caused by brain swelling rather than by an external force, received a similar level of criticism. One medical expert showed images of intracranial bleeding, but not the brain swelling that was supposed to have given rise to them. Consequently, the Court concluded that the unified hypotheses could not be regarded as a credible or alternative cause of the triad of injuries. Indeed, the presentation of the conflicting medical evidence led Geddes herself to concede that the unified hypothesis was nothing more than that, and in her view should not be used in court as evidence that a child died accidentally.

The Court also examined biomechanical evidence submitted by two experts to explain if violent shaking could result in forces causing the pathological symptoms evident in cases of alleged SBS. The experts reached different conclusions on the issue. The Court commented that '[Biomechanics] is a complex, developing and (as yet) necessarily uncertain area of science' (para 213(v)) and indicated that, where such evidence is called by one or other party or both in future litigation, it will be for the jury (in a criminal trial) or the judge (in a civil trial) to evaluate it in the light of cross examination and all the other evidence. Faris Bandak, who has published biomechanical research to address the question of the degree of force required to produce the triad of injuries in SBS, claims that although the legal system has to make judgements about the credibility of scientific evidence, there is a danger of marginalisation of certain types of evidence on the basis of opinion provided by a limited number of experts who happen to disagree. He argues that it would be a setback for our understanding of the mechanism for SBS to say that as a result of these two experts disagreeing, biomechanical evidence can't tell us anything (Bandak 2005).

So what is the solution to such medical controversies? According to doctors and the legal system, more research will resolve the problem of conflicting medical opinion. Thus, there is an assumption that greater clinical certainty will facilitate the legal process so that decisions are made with greater confidence. However, such a proposition also suggests that science is value free and objective. As we have witnessed in the case of SBS, more research on the mechanisms of injury has actually resulted in greater clinical controversy. We explore this further in Chapter 6, but to conclude this chapter, a final brief note is called for to substantiate this assertion.

Concluding remarks

Giddens (1991) refers to modern organisations, such as the healthcare and the legal system, as 'expert' systems, and distinguishes them from their function in pre-modern contexts by the increased 'reflexive monitoring' that they foster. Reflexive monitoring refers to the process by which experts redefine their role through a critical examination of their work and its function. In the case of medical experts, this will apply to the way that clinicians define their work and their knowledge base in the light of new information. One obvious example here would be the recent research carried out by Geddes and colleagues, as well as other research that challenges existing understanding of causation in cases of SBS. Giddens (1991) suggests that the reflexivity endemic to modernity undermines the certainty of knowledge, even scientific knowledge. Such reflexive monitoring often leads to the revision of established knowledge claims in the light of new information. In the case of the current controversy in SBS between medical experts advocating opposing views, the reflexive monitoring is evident in the debates that we have described above. These controversies have been played out on two distinct fronts: within the esoteric circle, using Fleck's (1935) analogy, between medical experts who have disagreed about the nature of 'causality' of intracranial bleeding, and more widely in the legal and public arena, where the debate has become politicised and consequently characterised by a rhetorical discourse. Experts need to maintain public trust and the legitimacy claims employed by both sides of the debate were partly intended to do just that. The decision of the Court of Appeal in *R v Harris and others* (2005), for instance, was partly based on a desire by the legal system to be perceived as delivering 'justice for the innocents', as one publication coined the outcome (Coghlan 2005, p.6). Similarly, the General Medical Council's attempt to remove Professor Sir Roy Meadow from the medical register for serious professional misconduct was another example of a case where it was believed that the public's trust in the medical profession had to be protected. It therefore seems that the maintenance of legitimacy and credibility was a primary objective of both decisions.

The second issue of importance is one based on professional jurisdictions, where research conducted on SBS will be partly influenced by the ensuing controversy that exists in this field, potentially fuelling further debate as new hypotheses are developed. Whereas previously, prior to the research of Geddes and colleagues, paediatricians were most influential over the definition of SBS and the causes of suspected NAHI in children, currently the playing field has become more populated. For instance, the current debate surrounding the causes of SBS incorporates a wider spectrum of participants, including neuropathology, radiology, as well as beyond the medical domain in areas such as biomechanics, each competing to offer answers for the uncertainty that clouds this area of research. Giddens (1991) suggests that the reflexivity endemic to modernity actually undermines the certainty of scientific knowledge, even in the core domains of natural science. A workspace is frequently forged by the moral discourses displayed by actors resulting from the reflexive monitoring of their action. Thus, rather than interpreting this situation as a set of circumstances where one group of clinicians competes for jurisdiction and displaces another group, Giddens proposes that a 'dialectic' relationship ensues where no single occupational group or profession has outright control over a sphere of work or a knowledge claim. Instead, the situation is in a constant state of flux and negotiation, as the debate progresses within the scientific community as well as in the public domain.

CHAPTER 6

Responding to Non-Accidental Head Injury: Changes and Challenges

In this chapter we focus on events which occurred in the early years of the twenty-first century with a view to anticipating the challenges to be faced in responding to cases of suspected non-acidental head injury (NAHI) in future years. In the first part of the chapter we examine the key legal and political responses to the judgement of the Court of Appeal in the case of Angela Cannings and consider the impact of these events for child protection and the prosecution of abusers. In the second, concluding part of the chapter, we turn our attention to what we believe will be the main challenges to be faced in the future in responding effectively to cases of suspected NAHI.

Disputed medical evidence: the legacy of Angela Cannings

In the previous chapter we considered medical controversies over the causation of head injuries in young children and the role of expert evidence from a sociological perspective. In this section we return to the topic of controversy between medical expert witnesses by considering its impact on legal proceedings following the case of Angela Cannings in 2004. This case occurred in the wake of growing concerns about potential miscarriages of justice following the decision of the Court of Appeal to quash the convictions of Sally Clark for murdering her two sons and the acquittal of Trupti Patel who was charged with murdering three of her children. Despite the persistent linking of these three cases in the media, in fact each case raised different issues. Sally Clark's appeal was concerned with controversial statistical evidence given by Professor Sir Roy Meadows and relevant information being withheld by Dr Williams, the Home Office pathologist and the acquittal of Trupti Patel was a jury verdict which decided no point of principle. It is only the case of Angela Cannings which focused primarily on disputes between medical experts and which hence requires detailed consideration in this context. Although on its facts *Cannings* was not directly concerned with NAHI, as we shall see, the judgement of the Court of Appeal in this case proved to be something of a watershed, having significant ramifications for cases of alleged NAHI where causation is disputed.

In 2002 Angela had been convicted of the murder of two of her children. The prosecution had alleged that she had smothered both children. Angela had claimed that the deaths were natural, even if unexplained, incidents which should be classified as Sudden Infant Death Syndrome (SIDS) or cot deaths. Thus the issue for the jury to determine was one of causation: were the deaths of either of the two children caused by the actions of Angela, or were they due to some other reason, albeit an unascertained reason? In convicting Angela of murder, the jury were clearly satisfied that the former explanation was the correct one. In January 2004 the Court of Appeal received 'significant and persuasive' fresh evidence which related to SIDS in general and to hereditary factors in Angela's family which pointed to a possible genetic cause of the deaths and which had not been before the jury. As a result of the fresh evidence the Court concluded that Angela's convictions were unsafe and quashed them. In giving judgement, the Court commented that, in the case of unexplained infant deaths, we are still at the frontiers of knowledge in many respects and gave the following guidance:

> [F]or the time being, where a full investigation into two or more sudden unexplained infant deaths in the same family is followed by a serious disagreement between reputable experts about the cause of death, and a body of such expert opinion concludes that natural causes, whether explained or unexplained, cannot be excluded as a reasonable (and not a fanciful) possibility, the prosecution of a parent or parents for murder should not be started or continued, unless there is additional cogent evidence, extraneous to the expert evidence…to support the conclusion that the infant, or where there is more than one death, one of the infants was deliberately harmed. In cases like the present, if the outcome of the trial depends exclusively, or almost exclusively on a serious disagreement between distinguished and reputable experts, it will often be unwise, and therefore unsafe, to proceed. (*R v Cannings* (2004) para 175)

The period immediately following the decision in *Cannings* was one of great uncertainty for all concerned with child protection. The judgement was deployed in many cases by the defence in criminal trials as authority for different arguments running along the lines that whenever there was a genuine conflict between reputable experts, the prosecution should not proceed, or the evidence of the prosecution witnesses should be disregarded. At the same time, local authorities were said to be concerned and confused as to the applicability of the judgement to their statutory duties under the Children Act 1989. Certainly, in the immediate aftermath of the judgement, there is clear evidence of an overly cautious reaction on the part of trial judges to cases involving disputed medical evidence – a reaction which had potentially serious implications for cases of NAHI.

Three months after the Court of Appeal had given its judgement in *Cannings*, Mark Latta was facing trial charged with the murder of his ten-week-old baby daughter Charlotte who, when she died, was found to have 32 fractures of the ribs, arms and legs, retinal haemorrhages and extensive brain damage (Woolcock 2004). The injuries sustained by her included the triad of injuries commonly associated with shaking and were clearly indicative of NAI, and so the judge ruled that it was beyond doubt that someone had abused Charlotte. However, as to the cause of *death*, he ruled that the prosecution had failed to exclude the chance that Charlotte's death had been due to vomit causing her throat to spasm, leading to a lack of oxygen to the brain and, influenced by the judgement in *Cannings*, he withdrew the case from the jury. Although the issue of *who* killed Charlotte was arguably problematic on the facts, it is difficult to see the relevance of *Cannings* to this case, not least because there was clearly 'additional cogent evidence…to support the conclusion that the infant…was deliberately harmed'. If the case had been left to jury it is, of course, possible that they would have been left with a reasonable doubt as to the cause of death, but withdrawing the case from the jury in this way was arguably indicative of an overly cautious reaction to *Cannings*.

The *Latta* case inevitably served to fuel concerns about the potential impact of the judgement in *Cannings* on cases involving disputed medical evidence and, for a time, it seemed that such knee-jerk reactions might become commonplace. However, subsequent decisions of the Court of Appeal indicate a more measured approach, limiting the effect of *Cannings* in both criminal prosecutions and child protection proceedings. For those who were concerned that Cannings would have a detrimental effect on their ability to protect abused children, the first sign of reassurance came from the Court of Appeal in May 2004 in the cases of *Re U; Re B* (2004) when the

Court concluded that the responsibilities of local authorities under the Children Act 1989 had not been changed by the decision in *Cannings*. In each case the threshold conditions in s 31 of the Children Act 1989 had been found to be established on the basis that the mothers had caused their child significant harm and the mothers sought permission to appeal, relying in part on the judgement in *Cannings*. In giving judgement in the two cases the Court of Appeal pointed out that the decision in *Cannings* turned on the very particular facts of the case and commented that there may have been a tendency in some quarters to overestimate the impact of the judgement in family proceedings (para 24). In fact, counsel for the mother in *Re B* had gone so far as to contend that, in cases where there is a serious disagreement between reputable experts leading to one opinion that natural causes could not be excluded as a reasonable possibility, then, absent clear extraneous evidence, care proceedings should not be issued – a submission which the Court of Appeal 'robustly rejected' (para 26). A similar message was given by the Court of Appeal the following year in relation to criminal trials. In the case of *R v Kai-Whitewind* (2005) the Court referred to the defence contention that where there is conflict of opinion between reputable experts, the expert evidence called by the Crown is automatically neutralised as the 'overblown *Cannings* argument' and said it was a startling proposition that was not sustained by *Cannings* itself (para 84).

Thus, it seems that the impact of *Cannings* has not been as great as initially anticipated. Immediately after the Court of Appeal gave its judgement in *Cannings*, the Attorney General had asked the Crown Prosecution Service to review all current cases where a parent or carer was being prosecuted for killing an infant under two and had also established a review of 297 similar cases which had resulted in a conviction in the previous ten years. Similarly, local authorities had been instructed to undertake a review of cases where victims and/or siblings had been taken into care on the basis of disputed medical evidence (Department for Education and Skills 2004b). The instigation of these reviews led to speculation in the media that 'hundreds' of other convictions would be quashed and that 'thousands' of children who had been taken into care on the basis of disputed medical evidence would be returned to their families. However, in November 2004 it was reported that of the 28,867 care cases reviewed, only 26 were found to have involved disagreement between experts about medical evidence and, of those, only five cases raised 'serious doubt' about the reliability of the evidence which led to the care order being made (Frith 2004). Similarly, in December 2004 the

Attorney General reported that of the 297 cases reviewed, only 28 were found to have questionable convictions (Attorney General 2004) and by January 2006 only two parents had had their convictions for killing their children quashed, leading to newspaper headlines asking 'So what happened to all the feared miscarriages of justice?' (Dyer 2006).

Despite this, the judgment in *Cannings* undoubtedly serves as a useful reminder of the need to scrutinise disputed medical evidence carefully, and perhaps its greatest legacy has been the refocusing of attention on the crucial role played by medical expert witnesses, particularly in areas where we are still at the frontiers of knowledge. As we have seen, NAHI is one such area and, as part of the review conducted by the Attorney General, 89 cases of NAHI were identified. Although these cases raised issues of causation where medical expertise is currently being developed, as in the case of SIDS, they can clearly be distinguished from *Cannings*, in that they involved no suggestion of SIDS or unexplained deaths. Despite this, the distinction has persistently been disregarded in the media and, as a result, SIDS and NAHI have been conflated in the minds of many. At the time of the initial review, the Attorney General decided to defer final consideration of the 89 cases of NAHI pending the decision in four cases which were due to be heard by the Court of Appeal. These cases were considered in July 2005 in a conjoined appeal, *R v Harris and others* (2005). The appellants appealed against their convictions for murder, manslaughter and inflicting grievous bodily harm (GBH). The common thread running through each of the four appeals was a submission that, since the conviction, medical research had developed to the extent that there was 'fresh evidence' which threw doubt on the safety of each conviction and as to the amount of force necessary to cause the injuries. One of the key pieces of evidence related to the research conducted by Geddes *et al.* (2001; 2003) which propounded a new hypothesis which challenged the supposed infallibility of the triad. The new 'unified hypothesis' suggested that the cause of the triad was not necessarily trauma but hypoxia, as we discussed in Chapter 5. In reviewing the evidence, the Court of Appeal held that the unified hypothesis could not be regarded as a credible or alternative cause of the triad. However, on the evidence before it, the Court found that presence of the triad did not *automatically* and *necessarily* lead to a finding of NAHI and that all the circumstances, including the clinical picture, had to be taken into account. The Court stressed that cases of NAHI are fact-specific and should be determined on their individual facts.

RESPONDING TO NON-ACCIDENTAL HEAD INJURY / 149

This point is well illustrated by a brief resume of the outcome of the four appeals.

1. Harris:

In the case of the first appellant, Harris, the prosecution had alleged she had shaken her son and she had been convicted of the manslaughter of her son. On appeal the defence produced evidence which suggested an alternative cause of death based on an infection, but the Court determined that this did not form any basis for holding that the conviction was unsafe. However, the triad stood alone and the clinical evidence pointed away from NAHI. Furthermore, the triad itself was uncertain as new evidence threw doubt on the significance of such subdural haemorrhage (SDH), and it also cast doubt on the evidence of injuries to the brain. Although the Court found that evidence of the findings of RH was powerful supporting evidence of shaking, on its own it was not sufficient to justify a finding of shaking. The Court concluded that the fresh evidence as to the cause of death and the amount of force necessary to cause the triad might reasonably have affected the jury's decision to convict and so the conviction was quashed.

2. Rock:

The second appellant, Rock, had been convicted of the murder of his partner's child. The Court of Appeal pointed out that this was not a case where the medical evidence and the presence of the triad stood alone. There was evidence that Rock had shown some hostility towards the child and there was no dispute that he had shaken the child and she had suffered an impact to the back of her head. Therefore, the Court concluded that on all the evidence, Rock's conviction for unlawful killing was safe. However, as we discussed in Chapter 4, the Court quashed the murder conviction and substituted a conviction for manslaughter on the basis that the level of force required to cause the injuries did not necessarily demonstrate the necessary culpability for murder.

3. Cherry:

In the case of the third appellant, Cherry, who had been convicted of the manslaughter of his partner's daughter, the decision for the jury had been whether they could be sure that the child's death was caused by an unlawful act on the part of Cherry, or whether her death might have been attributable to an accidental fall from a chair some six to eight inches high. Two elements of the triad were present and the Court found that Cherry's factual account could not explain the child's injuries and death as the postulated fall was not a credible cause, or contributory cause, of her death. Furthermore, there was also evidence of up to 22 bruises on the child's body. In all the circumstances, the Court decided that Cherry's conviction for manslaughter was safe and so dismissed his appeal.

4. Faulder:
In the final case, Faulder had been convicted of inflicting GBH on his son. At trial the prosecution had alleged that Faulder had shaken the child, but Faulder claimed that he had dropped his son by accident when placing him in his pushchair. On appeal, the defence introduced what the Court referred to as 'potentially credible alternative' explanations. However, perhaps the key factor which influenced the Court was the fact that, on appeal, the prosecution case had changed from allegations of shaking to allegations of multiple blows to the head. This led the Court to conclude that, despite the number of bruises found on the child's body, Faulder's conviction had to be considered unsafe and so it was quashed.

The judgement of the Court of Appeal in this case contains a detailed review of the key areas of conflict between medical expert witnesses on the issue of causation in cases of NAHI. It is also a model of clear and careful judicial reasoning which repays careful reading. But those hoping that the judgement would provide the 'answer' to any conflict between experts in a case of alleged NAHI are inevitably going to be disappointed, simply because there is no one 'answer' – at least, not at this moment in time. The message from the Court of Appeal in *R v Harris and others* (2005) is clear: each case is fact-specific and must be determined on its individual facts.

Following the judgement of the Court of Appeal, the Attorney General ordered a review of the 88 remaining NAHI cases which had previously been identified (by this time one of the original 89 cases had already been referred back to the Court of Appeal) and the results of this review were made available in February 2006 (Attorney General 2006). The first task of the reviewers had been to consider each of the 88 cases and identify those which required further, more detailed consideration. The Attorney General reported that in the majority of cases it had become clear that other extraneous evidence existed to support the finding of NAHI. Examples of such extraneous evidence included: admissions to shaking and punching the infant; earlier fractures; head injuries occurring on two separate occasions; earlier fractures indicating the infant had been squeezed violently and evidence that the infant had been struck against a wall causing catastrophic injuries. Only 10 of the 88 cases were found to merit further investigation and, of these 10 cases, the reviewers identified only 3 cases in which there was some concern over the safety of the convictions. Two of these related to convictions for manslaughter, where further medical investigations were suggested and one related to murder. However, this latter case did not involve medical considerations, but the question of the necessary intent for the offence. The review therefore concluded that the vast majority (85 of 88) cases did not give cause for concern, although, as the Attorney General pointed out, this conclusion did not prevent any of those whose cases had been reviewed from taking legal advice and, if appropriate, seeking leave to appeal out of time to the Court of Appeal.

To conclude this section, we must acknowledge that we do not know how many prosecutions have not proceeded, or indeed how many prosecutions have simply not been instigated in cases of suspected NAHI as a direct result of the initial furore following the case of *Cannings*. However, the results of the Attorney General's review indicate that, whatever the short-term impact may have been, the long-term legacy of *Cannings* is not to prevent prosecutions taking place, but to encourage a careful appraisal of the totality of the evidence in each case. This message has been reinforced by decisions of the Court of Appeal in both criminal and child protection cases, although, as we discussed in Chapter 4, in the latter cases the courts can draw on a wider range of evidence in coming to a decision.

Future challenges

As we have emphasised throughout this book, responding to cases of suspected NAHI in young children can be a complex and challenging task. Developments in the twenty-first century have arguably served only to increase the complexity of the task and, in this concluding section, we return to some of the issues we have discussed in previous chapters in order to examine what we believe are now the greatest challenges to be faced.

Investigation of suspected non-accidental head injury

We have already examined the inherent difficulties involved in identifying and protecting children who have been the victim of NAHI and in identifying and punishing the abuser. It is now also clear that each case is fact-specific, that the presence of the triad will not be sufficient to justify a finding of NAHI, and that science alone cannot always provide the answers we seek. Consequently, the quantity and quality of evidence gathered during the investigative process will be crucial if the miscarriages of justice are to be avoided yet children are to be protected from abuse and abusers are to be punished. As we discussed in Chapters 3 and 4, the starting point in the evidence-gathering process will frequently be the treating clinician when a child presents with injuries which are indicative of possible abuse and we have made recommendations in Chapter 3 relating to the role of clinicians in identifying abuse. Yet these initial investigations must be accompanied by referral, followed by a detailed and thorough investigation by both police and social services which must be complemented by seamless inter-agency co-operation throughout the investigative process. Whilst the changes to the delivery of children's services following the Children Act 2004 and the associated revisions to the Working Together guidance (which we discussed in Chapter 1) will hopefully enhance inter-agency co-operation in ensuring the well-being of all children, we must not lose sight of the need for an integrated approach to the reporting and investigation of suspected NAI, supported by a detailed protocol to address the specific issues which arise in cases of NAHI.

Encouraging clinicians to report suspected non-accidental injury

In Chapter 3 we discussed the clinical identification of non-accidental injury (NAI) and referred to the culture of under-reporting of suspected NAI amongst clinicians. We now return to this issue and consider what steps can be taken to encourage reporting once a suspicion has been formed. Unlike many European countries and the USA, the law in England and Wales does not provide for the compulsory reporting of suspected NAI in children. The possibility of introducing such a law was considered by an interdepartmental working party established as part of a review of child care law in 1985 (Department of Health and Social Security 1985), but the working group concluded that there was no demonstrable need for a reporting law, stressing that those professionals who may be covered by such a law were imbued by their training, tradition and character of their work with a strong emphasis on the welfare of children and their families. Furthermore, the group was of the opinion that the enactment of a mandatory duty might be counter-productive and increase the risk to children overall; first by weakening the individual professional's personal sense of responsibility and, second, in casting the shadow of near automatic reporting over their work which may raise barriers between clinicians and their patients. It was also thought that the imposition of a mandatory duty to report would set back the advances made over the years in encouraging communication and co-operation between all those concerned with the health and welfare of children. Given the advances in inter-agency co-operation since the working party considered the issue in 1985, it seems unlikely that further consideration will be given to the introduction of a mandatory duty to report in the foreseeable future.

Although clinicians are not under any legal duty to report suspicions, they can now rest assured that, as long as they are acting in good faith in what they believe to be the best interests of the child in reporting suspected abuse, they will not be subject to proceedings being brought against them by aggrieved parents if subsequent inquiries reveal the suspicions to be unfounded. In *D v East Berkshire Community Health NHS Trust* (2005) the House of Lords decided that there were cogent policy reasons why healthcare professionals, acting in good faith in the best interest of a child, should not be subject to potentially conflicting duties in deciding whether the child may have been abused or whether to report suspicions once formed. In ruling that no duty of care was owed in such circumstances, Lord Brown referred to two fundamental considerations:

> [F]irst, the insidious effect that his awareness of the proposed duty would have upon the mind and conduct of the doctor (subtly tending to the suppression of doubts and instincts which in the child's interest ought rather to be encouraged), and, second, a consideration inevitably bound up with the first, the need to protect him against the risk of costly and vexing litigation, by no means invariably soundly based. (para 137)

The decision of the House of Lords in this case sends a positive message to clinicians who suspect abuse and, when combined with the decision of the High Court in the case of Professor Sir Roy Meadow (which we discuss below), represents a significant step towards making the child protection process a more inviting arena into which clinicians can be encouraged to step. However, the extent to which this immunity from legal action and disciplinary proceedings will actively encourage clinicians to report suspicions may well be limited. As we discussed in Chapter 3, although the research evidence on clinical referral patterns is limited, it remains the case that it may well be 'easier' for a busy clinician to focus on treating the physical symptoms of abuse and, to adopt the terminology used by Lord Brown (above), 'to suppress doubts and instincts (about the cause of the injuries) which, in the child's interests, ought to be encouraged'.

Investigating non-accidental head injury: guidance, protocols and the correct starting point

In 2002, a study into the police investigation of shaken baby murders and assaults in the UK, which was undertaken for the Home Office under a Police Research Award Scheme, noted that there was a complete lack of training to deal with cases when children with head injuries were brought to a hospital and identified as having been abused (Wheeler and McDonagh 2002). The study aimed to take a snapshot of how such cases were being dealt with by police forces in the UK in 2002 and made suggestions as to good practice learned from the experience of investigating similar cases and from research efforts. The research conducted for the study also led to the development of a CD training package for police and social services personnel and an 'investigator's guide to investigating shaken baby syndrome cases' which aimed to help investigating officers understand the complexity of the cases and raise awareness of the thoroughness needed to obtain convictions. The study therefore constituted a significant step towards the development of an investigation protocol for suspected NAHI, recognising as it did that 'one of the keys to a successful investigation of this kind is to realise from the start that it is going to be a multi-disciplinary event in nature' (p.114). Although subsequent events, including the research by Geddes *et al.*, have cast doubt on some of the previously accepted medical 'certainties' relied on, the study nevertheless provides a useful framework for an investigation protocol for cases of suspected NAHI.

More detailed protocols have been developed in related areas. In 2003, following the cases of Sally Clark, Trupti Patel and Angela Cannings, the Presidents of the Royal College of Pathologists and the Royal College of Paediatrics and Child Health recognised the seriousness of the events that were unfolding and, even before the hearing of Angela Canning's successful appeal, established a working group to consider the implications of these cases for the medical profession. The group reported in September 2004 and produced a detailed, multi-agency protocol for care and investigation of sudden unexpected death in infancy (SUDI) (Royal College of Pathologists and the Royal College of Paediatricians and Child Health 2004). Although this protocol has been developed specifically for care and investigation in cases of SUDI, many of its recommendations concerning the multi-agency investigative process are relevant to the investigation of cases of suspected NAI, particularly when the child has died. For example, the protocol makes detailed recommendations as to the information to be collected by the paediatrician (Appendix II) and also contains an autopsy protocol for SUDI (Appendix III).

We would, however, express one note of caution. The basis of the protocol is the acknowledgement that in the vast majority of cases where babies suddenly die, nothing unlawful has taken place and it is therefore said to be essential that police start from the position that the vast majority of babies' deaths are from natural causes. The protocol acknowledges that for the police, this is hard to reconcile with modern training for criminal investigations, which emphasises the importance of 'the golden hour' – the first hour of evidence-gathering that produces crucial evidence before it can be lost or contaminated. The protocol suggests that the point that should be emphasised in police training is the statistical one that few cases of SUDI should be cause for suspicion, which should arise only if there is material evidence of something irregular, such as medical evidence of injury or evidence of concern from social services or police child protection unit records. Thus the starting point for the protocol is the presumption that the child's death is natural. Whilst statistical evidence and current scientific knowledge of SUDI justify such an approach, cases in which a child has sustained head injuries need to be distinguished from SUDI. As we have seen, research by Jayawant *et al.* (1998) indicates that abuse is the commonest cause of head injuries in young children and so, even if there is a genuine dispute as to how the injuries were caused, a presumption that an innocent explanation for the injuries will be forthcoming cannot be justified on the basis of statistical evidence and furthermore would have a detrimental impact on the subsequent investigation.

Pushing back the frontiers of knowledge – the urgent need for more research
As we have seen, although forensic science is often portrayed as an infallible discipline and it is frequently assumed that science will always provide definite answers, in reality scientific evidence is rarely such a neatly packaged entity. Advances in scientific knowledge and expertise are continually being made and, as the Court of Appeal pointed out in *R v Cannings* (2004) (para 156), it is inevitable that these advances will sometimes create doubt about what were once thought to be certainties. Indeed, the medical controversy over the cause of head injuries in young children (which we examined in

Chapter 5) is a classic example of how scientific knowledge and expertise evolve over time, thereby throwing doubt on explanations which were once accepted without question. The inevitable consequence of such development is that miscarriages of justice, such as that in the case of Angela Canning, will be uncovered. If further research into SIDS and the role played by genetic factors in unexplained infant deaths had not been undertaken, Angela's conviction for killing her two children would not have been quashed. However, the new scientific evidence did not itself *cause* the miscarriage of justice, which had taken place when Angela was initially convicted; it merely uncovered it. Without the new evidence, an even greater miscarriage of justice would have occurred, albeit unknown. But this does not, of course, mean that the scientific evidence should not have been admitted in the first trial. Whilst we must accept that later research may well prove current theories wrong, as Keogh (2004) points out, this should not lead to the exclusion of scientific evidence as to do so would deny the justice system of a valuable contribution to current thinking.

Although we have advocated throughout this book that a wide range of evidence should be taken into account in reaching decisions in cases of suspected NAHI and we have argued against undue reliance on medical evidence alone, the fact remains that medical evidence is inevitably the cornerstone on which many allegations of NAHI are based. As more specialised sciences are established, it may be that science poses more questions than it solves – in 2002, it was pointed out that the research by Geddes *et al.* had posed questions in the field of SDH in young children, but it had not provided answers (*Re A and D (Non Accidental Injury: Subdural Haematomas)* (2002) para 41). Yet, as Wilson (2005) points out, if we do not venture into areas of disputed science, we fail to protect the most vulnerable members of society. Therefore, whilst we must guard against expecting science to provide us with the answer to all of our problems, further scientific research is vital if miscarriages of justice are to be avoided and children are to be effectively protected. This may well be a daunting task, both from an objective, scientific perspective and from a more personal one. In relation to the former, advances in scientific knowledge can be achieved through painstaking research, utilising a wide variety of clinical, laboratory, biochemical, biomechanical, pathological and animal research models that address these central forensic issues, from a variety of different perspectives. Although this may appear to be a daunting task, it can be achieved, as Hymel (2005) suggests, 'one small step at a time' (p.946). In relation to the latter, the recent vilification of previously eminent expert witnesses (which we discuss below) has led to concerns that researchers will be less interested in studying child abuse, despite it being a subject which is in urgent need of scientific attention (Horton 2005).

The provision of scientific evidence to the courts: the expert witness

We have acknowledged that forensic science is not an infallible discipline and there are intrinsic weaknesses in forensic evidence. Yet, social utility requires the admission of medical expert evidence in cases of suspected NAHI, despite its potential unreliability. There has been a tendency in the media to attribute the failure of forensic testimony in high profile cases solely to individual experts. Whilst this is arguably too simplistic, as it fails to take account of the weaknesses which are inherent in forensic evidence, it is true that these underlying weaknesses are frequently exacerbated by the failings on the part of the individual who provides this evidence – the expert witness – and it is to this issue which we now turn.

The reluctant witness

For several years there have been growing concerns about the reluctance of paediatricians to become involved in child protection work and the diminishing number of professionals who are prepared to give expert evidence in child abuse cases (Kmietowicz 2004; Thorpe 2006). The prospect of a shortage of professionals willing to give expert evidence is generally thought to represent a difficulty for the prosecution or for the local authorities in child abuse cases, although, as Gooderham (2005, p.4) points out, it may have a greater adverse effect upon parents suspected of harming their children, many of whom have significantly limited funding. These concerns have been exacerbated following the cases of Sally Clark and Angela Cannings and in June 2004 the government announced an initiative, to be led by Sir Liam Donaldson, the Chief Medical Officer, to determine how best to ensure the availability of medical expert resources to the family courts (Thorpe 2006). However, subsequent events arguably served to undermine confidence in the provision of expert evidence to the courts still further and, for a time, it seemed that the concerns were leading towards a major crisis in this area. In July 2005, in what had been described as a 'grievously erroneous decision' (Horton 2005, p.277), Professor Sir Roy Meadow was found guilty of serious professional misconduct and struck off the Medical Register by the Fitness to Practice Panel (FPP) of the General Medical Council (GMC) for giving misleading expert evidence in the case of Sally Clark. A month earlier Home Office pathologist Dr Alan Williams had been found guilty of serious professional misconduct for not disclosing key evidence in the same case and also for errors in the conclusions he drew from post-mortem evidence. Both men were vilified in the media, both before and after the determinations of the GMC. Even before Sir Roy was struck off the Medical Register, a House of Commons Select Committee (House of Commons 2005a) noted that the treatment of his case in the media had had many ramifications, one of which was the increasing reluctance of experts to risk their reputation by appearing as expert witnesses. Following the GMC's determination, Horton (2005) claimed that the decision would leave a deeply damaging footprint over child protection in the UK, which would influence the interests of children for years to come. However, in February 2006 the High Court gave the first glimmer of hope to those concerned with averting the growing crisis. Sir Roy appealed against the decision of the GMC and, in allowing his appeal, the High Court delivered a judgement which has implications far beyond the case itself.

In law, it has long been recognised that a witness has immunity from suit in respect of evidence he or she gives in a court of law. The immunity, which extends to the honest as well as the dishonest witness, is based on public policy which requires that a witness should not be deterred from giving evidence by fear of litigation instigated by those who may feel that the evidence has damaged them unjustifiably and it is therefore in the interests of the judicial process that a witness should not be exposed to the risk of having his or her evidence challenged in another process. It applies as much to an expert as to any other witness and it was therefore clear that Sir Roy was immune from a civil action in respect of the matters alleged against him in the disciplinary proceedings before the GMC. In hearing his appeal against the ruling of the GMC, the High Court considered the question whether immunity from suit should be extended to provide immunity from disciplinary proceedings. Collins J concluded that, given the rationale underlying the rule on immunity, not only was there no reason in principle why it should not apply to disciplinary proceedings, but there was every reason why it *should* so apply. As he commented, 'There can be no doubt that the administration of justice has been seriously damaged by the decision of FPP (in the case of Sir Roy) and the damage will continue unless it is made clear that such proceedings need not be feared by the expert witness' (*Meadow v General Medical Council* (2006), para 19). Although the court recognised that absolute immunity was not justified, the result of the judgement is that experts can give evidence free from the fear of subsequent disciplinary action unless they act so contrary to their obligations to their profession and to the court that the court decides to make a complaint.

Therefore, following this judgement, the only circumstances in which disciplinary proceedings based on evidence given by an expert in court can be brought are those when the *court* makes a complaint to the expert's professional body. This conclusion was, of course, sufficient to ensure the success of Sir Roy's appeal as the FPP should not have considered the initial complaint, which had been made by the father of Sally Clark. But, in case the court's conclusion on immunity was subject to a further appeal, the court also went on to consider the appeal on the basis that the FPP had been entitled to consider the complaint and concluded that, on the evidence before it, the FPP had not been justified in finding Sir Roy guilty of serious professional misconduct. Indeed, Collins J commented 'It is difficult to think that the giving of honest albeit mistaken evidence could save in an exceptional case properly lead to such a finding' (para 56). The judgement in this case therefore sends a reassuring message to potential expert witnesses. It is also indicative of the courts' clear desire to protect experts and ameliorate the damaging impact of events in recent years on the provision of expert evidence to the courts. It is to be hoped that this trend will continue.

In March 2006 the GMC announced its intention to seek permission to appeal against the High Court ruling on immunity (Hawkes 2006). The GMC acknowledged that there is a problem to be solved, and that it cannot be in the public interest if doctors are deterred from giving evidence, honestly and truthfully, and within their competence, but claimed that the solution does not lie in extending the principle of immunity in a 'wholly novel way' thereby placing doctors and other professionals beyond the reach of their regulator. Whatever the outcome of any appeal made by the GMC, every effort must be made not only to ensure the continuing availability of medical expert resources to the courts but also to ensure that the evidence provided is of the required high standard and based on scientific research and that, in areas of dispute, it is subjected to rigorous testing and examination. These aims can be achieved, at least in part, through effective regulation, accreditation and training of expert witnesses and possibly by more wide-ranging procedural reforms to address failures in the system, as opposed to failures by individual experts.

Accreditation and assessing the competence of experts

As we discussed in Chapter 5, the purpose of expert evidence is to provide a court with information based on scientific expertise, the interpretation of which is outside the experience and knowledge of the judge and, where relevant, the jury. It is the court's responsibility to decide whether there is a need for expert evidence and also to establish the competency of any expert witness called, but the choice of which expert to instruct is generally a matter for the party wishing to call the witness. In order to assist the parties and the court in their respective tasks of choosing which expert witness to instruct and assessing the competence of the witness to act as an expert, several organisations maintain databases or registers with varying degrees of rigour determining eligibility for entry. These include: the Society of Expert Witnesses; the Academy of Experts; the Expert Witness Institute; the Law Society; the UK Register of Expert Witnesses and the Council for the Regulation of Forensic Practitioners (CRFP). Although it has been argued that accreditation schemes act only to usurp the role of professional bodies and the courts as arbitrators of who is fit to provide expert evidence (Pamplin 2004), efforts are continually being made to encourage experts to become accredited. For example, in publicly funded cases, the Legal Services Commission is seeking to encourage solicitors to use accredited expert witnesses who are on the register maintained by the CRFP (Legal Services Commission 2004). However, registration and accreditation remain voluntary for those acting as expert witnesses. As the CRFP itself has commented:

> In a free society no one should seek to constrain the courts as to the evidence they can hear; and there will always be situations where evidence is required from an expert in a very small speciality or one whose expertise is needed in court too rarely to justify maintaining a registration scheme. (House of Commons 2005a, para 137)

Furthermore, the mere inclusion of an individual's name on a list of experts may not be sufficient for the specific aspects of a particular case and, conversely, many individuals not listed on a register or database may nevertheless be sufficiently qualified and experienced to act as an expert witness. Therefore, despite increasing opportunities for registration and accreditation, assessing the competence of a witness to give expert evidence remains, at present, a matter solely for the court.

In 2004 the report on SUDI (Royal College of Pathologists and the Royal College of Paediatricians and Child Health 2004) advised that, before a doctor gives evidence as an expert, the court should establish his or her status and credentials by using the following prompts:

- What is the expert's area of practice?
- Is the doctor still in practice?
- What is the doctor's area of expertise?
- To what extent is the witness an expert in the subject to which the doctor testifies?
- When did the doctor last see a case in their own clinical practice?
- Is the doctor in good standing with their medical Royal College?
- Is the doctor up-to-date with continuing professional development?
- Has the doctor received training in the role of the expert witness in the last five years? (We discuss the issue of training below.)
- To what extent is the doctor's view widely held?

These prompts are clearly applicable to those offering expert evidence in cases of NAHI in both the family and criminal courts and the Academy of Medical Royal Colleges, whose objectives are to co-ordinate the work of the Medical Royal Colleges and Faculties, has recommended that these tests should be applied to medical expert witnesses in all situations (Academy of Medical Royal Colleges 2006).

Training for expert witnesses

In many respects, expert witnesses have an unenviable task. They are frequently expected to translate extremely complex and voluminous scientific evidence into evidence which can be understood by lay people, whether a judge or jury. Furthermore, this must be done within the relatively foreign environment of the courtroom which, as Wilson (2005) points out, is demanding and asserts tremendous pressure on experts to answer questions. Although some useful guidance is available for expert witnesses in Children Act cases (Wall 2000), the Select Committee on Science and Technology (House of Commons 2005a) expressed the view that training of all expert witnesses in the general principles of presentation of evidence to courts and the legal process is essential and recommended that the Department for Constitutional Affairs (DCA) should make funding available for expert witnesses who would otherwise not receive such training to ensure that they do have access to such training in advance of their appearance in court (para 144). The government's response was unequivocal: 'We do not accept that the DCA should be responsible for funding the training of experts. Such training is the responsibility of the professions to which expert witnesses belong, and a variety of training in this area is already available' (House of Commons 2005b, p.14). Whilst it is true that several of the organisations to which expert witnesses belong, such as the Academy of Experts and the Expert Witness Institute, do offer training programmes to maintain and enhance standards and the status of their members, the lack of any accredited training programme and associated government funding is a matter of concern. Furthermore, the report on SUDI (Royal College of Pathologists and the Royal College of Paediatricians and Child Health 2004) recommended that any training should be renewed at least every five years, which, if accepted, can only exacerbate the problem of funding. As we have seen, the evidence presented by expert witnesses is frequently crucial to the outcome of a case. If this evidence is to be presented with the required honesty, integrity and impartiality, it is vital that the experts in question have access to accredited training programmes so that they understand the legal process and their role within it.

'Systems failure' and procedural reforms

In recent years, much of the criticism of expert evidence in the media has focused on individual experts and, as we have seen, this has had a detrimental impact on the willingness of other experts to serve as witnesses. However, it has also been pointed out that the pillorying of individual experts detracts attention from the flaws in the court process and legal system which, if addressed, could help prevent future miscarriages of justice (House of Commons 2005a, para 170). The increasing complexity of scientific evidence presented to the courts has certainly been one factor influential in generating proposals for procedural reform and, in addition to recommendations relating to the training of expert witnesses themselves, it has been suggested that mandatory training in the area of forensic evidence be introduced and that judges be given an annual update on scientific developments of relevance to the courts (House of Commons 2005a, paras 170–180). Some would argue that more extreme measures are required. Mahendra (2005) is of the view that it is now clear that a court, including a jury, is not the appropriate forum for thrashing out the differences in scientific opinion and that the means must be found for a multidisciplinary pre-trial – even pre-prosecution – review of the medical evidence in such cases. Mahendra suggests that the safest course, as far as it is possible to do so, is to ensure that a jury gets to hear only a consensus view of the scientific evidence. As we saw in Chapter 5, the provision of expert evidence in civil trials is governed by Part 35 of the Civil Procedure Rules (CPR), which aims to control the volume, impartiality and quality of evidence of experts and which, inter alia, give judges in the civil courts the power to appoint a single expert witness. Cases involving complex medical evidence can result in a proliferation of expert witnesses and so the appointment of a single expert by the court may be advantageous in controlling the volume of expert evidence. However, the courts have made it clear that, where certain evidence is pivotal to the judge's decision and by its very nature is not easily receptive to a challenge in the absence of any other expert opinion, the court should be slow to decline an application for a second expert (*Re W (a child) (non-accidental injury: expert evidence)* (2005)).

The provision of expert evidence in criminal trials is not currently subject to the same controls. Numerous recommendations have been made over the last 25 years (House of Commons 2005a; Royal College of Pathologists and the Royal College of Paediatricians and Child Health 2004; Royal Commission on Criminal Justice 1993) and in October 2005 the Criminal Procedure Rules Committee of the DCA published draft criminal procedure rules about expert evidence for consultation which are consciously modelled on equivalent civil rules in the CPR and which provide explicitly for pre-trial discussion between experts to identify areas of agreement and disagreement and so save court time (Department for Constitutional Affairs 2005). Most controversially, the draft criminal procedure rules contain provision for the criminal courts to appoint a single expert. The Criminal Procedure Rules Committee recognise that this is likely to be a controversial proposal and explain that the intention is that the discretion should be exercised sparingly and where the expert's conclusions are not expected to be in dispute (para 16). Certainly, in cases involving disputed allegations of abuse where there is conflicting medical evidence on the issue of causation, a defendant could never be denied the right to instruct his or her own expert witness. Indeed, in the absence of an agreement between the parties, it is difficult to envisage any circumstances in which the appointment by a criminal court of a single expert would survive a challenge under article 6 of the European Convention on Human Rights, which guarantees the right to a fair trial.

More positive steps have been taken in relation to the disclosure of unused material by expert witnesses. As a result of the growing concern among practitioners and the public at the way in which the criminal law deals with issues surrounding expert evidence the Attorney General announced new guidance that focuses on the requirements made on expert witnesses in terms of disclosure (Crown Prosecution Service 2006). The guidance sets out what is required of expert witnesses, including the need to reveal to the investigator all the material they will have created in working on a case. Experts are now also required to certify that they have revealed to the prosecution any information that might adversely affect their credibility or competence as an expert witness and are reminded that they must not give expert opinion beyond their area of expertise. It is hoped that these guidelines will assist in bringing about greater confidence in the criminal justice system in handling difficult cases where expert witnesses provide evidence to the courts.

Whereas judges in the family courts have the opportunity to build up a certain amount of expertise in relation to the issues on which expert evidence may be given, criminal trials are more problematic in that the issues must be determined by a jury, the members of which are unlikely to have any relevant expertise. Furthermore, as Wilson (2005) points out, medical science is becoming increasingly more specialised and members of the jury no longer listen to two experts and decide whose testimony they prefer. The jury now has to weigh one scientific discipline against another scientific discipline, which is perhaps not something which may be performed with any degree of certainty, let alone by non-scientists in a trial setting. Concerns over the ability of jurors to understand complex medical evidence led Graham Zellick, chairman of the Criminal Cases Review Commission, to suggest that in the most difficult cases, the judge, perhaps with two medical scientists as assessors, should hear the expert evidence in the absence of the jury and then direct the jury on what to make of it, just as judges now direct juries on the law applying to a case (Dyer 2005b). Although such a scheme would have to be carefully thought out in order to comply with the right to a fair trial, the suggestion certainly has potential and those who are sceptical about the need for such a measure would be well advised to read (and endeavour to comprehend fully) the medical evidence presented to the Court of Appeal in the case of *R v Harris and others* (2005) before condemning the proposal out of hand.

Concluding comment

Our research findings made a significant contribution to the existing knowledge about NAHI in young children and since we concluded the research in 2002 we have followed subsequent events with interest. Despite radical changes to the delivery of children's services, new scientific research and the growing crisis in the provision of expert evidence, we believe that our research findings remain relevant today and, indeed, the findings have been of invaluable assistance to us throughout this book in our analysis of more recent events. Further research is urgently required, but we hope that our contribution to the debate will foster a clearer understanding of the issues involved and inform policy and practice in this area, thereby helping to ensure the most appropriate medical, legal and social responses to NAHI in young children.

The Research Project

This appendix summarises the methodology and findings of a two-year research project on the legal and social consequences which arise when children sustain a subdural haemorrhage (SDH). The research was funded by the Nuffield Foundation and undertaken by a multidisciplinary research team from the Family Studies Research Centre, which was set up to promote research collaboration between Cardiff University and the University of Wales College of Medicine (the institutions have now merged).

Aims and objectives of the research

- To identify the quantity and quality of evidence recorded in cases when a SDH is found on neuro imaging or at post mortem in a child under the age of two.

- To identify the number of cases where a child protection referral is made and/or a criminal prosecution is commenced and to ascertain the outcome of any such proceedings.

- To identify the factors which influence decisions to make a child protection referral or commence a criminal prosecution and to evaluate the impact of the available evidence on the outcome of any such proceedings with a view to assisting clinical and legal practice.

- To inform professionals as to the form and content of evidence required for medical records, child protection and criminal proceedings, thereby improving the evidential preparation of cases.

- To examine the long-term social and legal consequences for the families of infants who sustained a SDH in infancy, including any subsequent child protection referrals in relation to the victim and/or siblings.

- To heighten awareness of SDH amongst professionals and the public, to educate carers on the safe and proper handling of young children and to investigate the potential for future prevention.

The research methodology

The research was undertaken on a cohort of 68 children under the age of two who had sustained a SDH between 1992 and 1998 in Wales and South West England. The study was limited to Wales and the South West of England due to established contacts with paediatricians in this geographical area. This study was linked to an ongoing research investigation at the University of Wales College of Medicine, where a database on suspected physical injury in children was being developed, in order to identify the social and medical characteristics of children with suspected non-accidental injury (NAI) in Wales and the South West of England. It was decided that the volume of work required to extend the study to other geographical areas would be too great. In addition, as this study was exploratory in its aims, we did not need to reach a specific sample size.

The cases were identified from ICD-9 (International Classification of Diseases, 9th revision) inpatient coding, from admission books of hospital paediatric wards and from contact with paediatricians, neurosurgeons, pathologists, the coroner's office, and expert witnesses in child protection cases. Notifications of SDH (secondary to child abuse) in Wales were also identified through the Welsh Paediatric Surveillance System database. The 68 cases were selected from a total of 90 children under the age of two years, who had been admitted to hospital with a head injury. On close examination of the hospital notes, 22 cases were excluded from the study because a medical cause for the injuries was diagnosed. Subsequently, a further 14 cases were excluded from the study where a child protection referral had not been made. The study was only concerned with the cases that raised clinical suspicion of NAI. We were finally left with a total sample of 54 cases where there was a clinical suspicion of non-accidental head injury (NAHI). The relevant Research Ethics Committees granted ethical approval and in each case the medical records were accessed. In cases where a child protection referral had been made, access was negotiated to social service records and, where relevant, to the court records. Access was also negotiated to police records, Crown Prosecution Service and the Crown Court, where relevant. Key data from the various records in each case were identified, extracted and entered on one of four data collection schedules designed for the study (child protection, police, civil and criminal courts). Each case was given a unique identifier so that personal details could not be identified. To maintain complete confidentiality, all the data was coded numerically using a closed format system where textual information could not be entered, making case identification impossible. The data were subsequently analysed using the Statistical Package for Social Sciences (SPSS).

The research project was an exploratory study that was essentially a hypothesis generating, rather than a hypothesis testing, exercise. The case series methodology was adopted as it was decided that data collection, using a survey approach with professionals or carers, would not be feasible and personal interviews with carers would not be possible on ethical grounds. Inevitably, we encountered some practical problems with the collection of data. Not all files could be retrieved. We also discovered that some records (for example, the records of the Crown Prosecution Service (CPS) are routinely destroyed after a specified time, causing problems for a retrospective research study such as this. Despite these problems, the research resulted in a very rich collection of data relating to the cases in the study cohort.

Overview of results

Background characteristics of the 54 children in the study cohort where there was suspicion of non-accidental injury

Victims

Of the 54 children who were referred to police and social services, 38 were males and 16 were females. The age range was between 0.5 and 23 months, and the mean age was 5.4 months. Fourteen of the 54 children died following their injury. The age distribution of deceased children follows a similar pattern to the general age trend for the whole sample. These findings confirm studies carried out in the USA, which have reported fatality rates of between 23 per cent and 50 per cent in cases of suspected NAHI and found that boys were almost twice as likely to be victims as girls with the majority of victims being under 6 months of age (Starling *et al.* 1995).

The parents/carers

The children lived predominantly in two-parent families. In total, 43 children lived with both natural parents, 7 lived with their biological mother and her partner, and 4 lived only with the mother. The age distribution of mothers ranged between 17 and 39, with 57.4 per cent aged 25 or below. The age distribution of fathers was between 18 and 58, with 42.6 per cent aged 25 or below. In 7 cases the mother was cohabiting with a partner, whose age range was between 18 and 31, with 50 per cent aged 25 or below. When compared to the national mean age of parents of newly born babies, the mothers and their partners were much younger than the national mean age, although the fathers' age reflected the national mean.

Occupational class

The social position of the mother, father and the mother's partner was based on their occupational status. This provided a broad measure of social standing. Each parent/guardian was categorised according to their occupation at the time the SDH was detected. The occupational class of the parents was strongly skewed towards the lower end of the scale, where most carers held jobs in unskilled, partly skilled and skilled manual professions. A large number of parents lived in households where unemployment and material deprivation were common.

Social history

Social services records were examined for data of the parents' social history. In particular, information was recorded on alcohol or drug abuse, physical or mental illness including post-natal depression, a history of violence in current or past relationships (or experiencing violence), physical abuse in childhood, placement in care as a child, and previous child protection concerns. Mental illness, drug and alcohol abuse were relatively common among mothers and fathers. It was evident that seven mothers had experienced physical abuse in childhood, five had a care placement in the past, nine had post-natal depression following the birth of the (injured) child and in eight cases the social services had registered previous child protection concerns. Not as many social problems were identified among fathers and partners, possibly because a significant proportion of male carers were absent at the time of social services intervention.

Clinical intervention

Coexisting injuries

The child was found to have coexisting injuries, most of which were considered to be non-accidental, in 44 of the 54 cases which were referred. The injuries included fractures and/or bruises. Retinal haemorrhages were present in 36 cases.

Medical opinion

Information on medical opinion was drawn from reports written by clinicians who either had direct contact with the child during admission to hospital, or who were invited to provide an expert opinion to support child protection and legal procedures. Up to five medical opinions were offered in any one case. The opinion of clinicians was grouped according to the degree to which they believed that the SDH was as a result of NAI, where 1 represented definite NAI and 7 represented definitely not NAI. The mean opinion in each case ranged from 1.5 to 2.49, where 1 represents definite, 2 is probable and 3 is possible NAI, showing that clinicians felt that NAI was definite, probable or possible in most cases. A conflict of medical opinion during the child's admission to hospital as to the cause of the SDH was recorded in 10 of the 54 cases where a child protection referral was made.

'Referrals' versus 'non-referrals'

Out of the total study cohort of 68 children, no referral was made to the police or social services in 15 cases. The 'referrals' came from a lower socio-economic group than the 'non-referrals'; they were likely to be significantly younger and much more likely to come from families where the parents were unmarried than in the 'non-referral' cohort. The non-referred cases included recognised medical causes of SDH and witnessed major accidental injury in 12 cases. In retrospect 3 cases warranted referral.

Child protection process

Referral to social services

In cases where the child was referred to social services 95 per cent were referred within six days of admission, with 20 being referred on the day of admission, 9 within one day of admission, 7 within two days, and 4 within three days.

Registration

A case conference was convened following referral in 47 cases. In the 7 cases where no conference was convened, this was either because the child was dead or because the agencies did not perceive that there was a future threat to the child as the suspected perpetrator was no longer living with the child. The child was placed on the child protection register following the first case conference in 38 cases.

Risk assessment

A risk assessment was conducted in 39 cases. In 9 cases a risk assessment had not been conducted because the child had died, and in 6 cases there was no risk assessment because the suspected perpetrator either admitted causing the injuries and/or because they were no longer living with the victim, hence presenting no further risk. The mean time between the date of admission to hospital and the risk assessment was 8.7 months. Following a risk assessment the victims were most likely to be returned to both parents or placed in temporary foster care with a view to their being returned to their families in due course. Only a small minority of the victims were placed with relatives or adopted. The data support the hypothesis that the main objective following the risk assessment was for the rehabilitation of children with their families whenever possible. This reflects one of the principles underlying the Children Act 1989 – that children are best brought up in their own home with both parents playing an active role. However, this is a potentially problematic area as it was not clear how the risks of future abuse were assessed. It is possible that victims were rehabilitated with their families as it was believed that the risk of a further SDH diminished as the child grew older. This view is supported by the fact that, although a care order was made in respect of the victim in 14 cases, only one elder sibling was also made the subject of a care order.

Parental explanation for cause of injury

The most common response offered by parents when asked how the injury could have occurred was to provide no explanation. The second most common response was to claim that the child had an accident. Other responses included blaming the partner, blaming a sibling or blaming birth complications. A direct admission of shaking was made to social workers in only four cases. A subjective assessment of the level of co-operation of the carers with the social workers was made, based on the information contained in the records. It was evident that many carers were seen as being co-operative even in the absence of a direct admission, and the study revealed a strong negative relationship between the level of parental co-operation with social services and the decision to apply for a care order.

Police investigation

Referral to police

In 70.6 per cent of cases a referral was made to the police within two days of admission to hospital, and in 58.8 per cent a referral was made within one day. The general pattern of referral times is very similar to the pattern of referrals to social services. The overall mean time between admission to hospital and referral to police was 2.55 days, which is slightly longer than the equivalent mean referral time to social services (1.98 days), suggesting that the initial referral was usually made to a social worker. In all cases the police investigation was started on the day of referral.

The suspects

The most likely suspected perpetrators were the parents. In total 40 first (prime) suspects and 32 second suspects were interviewed by the police. The mean time between the date of admission to hospital and the interview by police for suspect 1 was 12.2 days, and 9.9 days for suspect 2. One or more suspects were arrested in 34 of the cases. The arrested suspects included 25 fathers, 20 mothers, 5 partners of the mother and 1 childminder.

Explanations for injuries to the police

The most common explanation at the first interview of the suspect was to deny knowledge of how the injury was caused or to blame an accident. This pattern of explanations reflected that offered by the parents at the case conference. Overall ten suspects admitted at some stage during the police investigations to having shaken the child, four during the first police interview, five during a second interview and one during a third interview. All suspects who admitted to having shaken the child were charged with one or more criminal offences, indicating that an admission was an important piece of evidence in building the prosecution case.

Charge

One or more charges were made in 25 cases. Twenty-one males and eight females were charged, with joint charges being brought in four cases. Thus the male carer was almost four times more likely to be charged than the mother. In total three suspects were charged with murder, three were charged with manslaughter, 11 were charged with causing grievous bodily harm (GBH) with intent, eight were charged with inflicting GBH, two were charged with actual bodily harm (ABH) and two were charged with assault. In five cases a charge of neglect (on the basis of failing to seek appropriate medical assistance for the child) under s 1 of the Children and Young Persons Act 1933 was brought in addition to the specific offences relating to the NAHI. This appeared to be used as a 'fall back' offence on which the prosecution could rely if they failed to prove beyond all reasonable doubt that the suspect was responsible for causing the injury.

Family proceedings

Proceedings were initiated in the family courts in 16 cases. A care order was applied for and granted in 13 cases and two supervision orders were applied for and granted. A care order application was unsuccessful in only one case, where, although the threshold criteria in s 31 of the Children Act 1989 had been

satisfied, by the time of the final hearing the order was not deemed to be necessary in the best interests of the child. Court records could be traced in only 9
out of the 16 cases. Two of these cases were concluded in the family proceedings court, 4 were transferred to care centres in the county court and 3 were
transferred to the High Court due to the complexity of the case. No interim
orders were deemed necessary in 2 of the cases where the victim was being
accommodated by the local authority. In the remaining 7 cases, between 3 and
11 interim care orders were made before the case was concluded.

Care plans

The care plan proposed by the local authority involved the long-term placement of the child with both parents in seven cases, placement of the child in
foster care in one case and adoption of the child in one case. This reflects the
position following the risk assessment in those cases which did not proceed to
the family courts (see above). Previous research has also found that returning
the child to parental care (reflecting the Children Act emphasis on this principle) is the most common plan following care proceedings (Hunt and Macleod
1999). However, although the number of cases analysed in this part of our
study was very small, the percentage of care plans involving return to parental
care is noticeably higher in cases where a child has sustained a SDH than in previous, more general, research studies and may reflect professional perceptions
of the risk of further abuse. Furthermore, although eight of the nine children
had elder siblings, only one sibling was made the subject of a care order, which
suggests that elder children are not thought to be at risk.

Expert medical evidence in the family courts

In total 40 medical witnesses provided expert evidence relating to the cause of
the injuries in the 9 cases. These were predominantly paediatricians (19), radiologists (9) and paediatric neurologists (3). (Seven other clinicians gave
evidence which was not specific to the cause of the injuries.) There was a greater
degree of consensus amongst the experts in court than there had been during
the child's admission to hospital (see above). Only one expert was uncertain as
to the cause of the injury, one thought it was probably not NAI and one thought
it was definitely not NAI (the latter two experts had both been instructed by the
parents). The remaining 37 experts thought the injury was definitely (12),
probably (23) or possibly (2) NAI.

Criminal trials

Due to the destruction of records we 'lost track' of seven cases after charge and it was only possible to view files in 13 cases which resulted in a trial on indictment. In five of these cases the defendant was the victim's mother, in seven cases the defendant was the victim's father and in one case the defendant was the partner of the victim's mother. The average length of time taken for a case to reach trial was 10.3 months from the date of the victim's admission to hospital. The length of trial varied between one and 15 days, with an average trial length of 3.6 days.

Guilty pleas

Seven of the 13 defendants entered a guilty plea at arraignment to one or more of the offences charged. Thus no trial was necessary. In one case the defendant pleaded guilty to manslaughter, in five cases the defendant pleaded guilty to one or more charge of inflicting GBH on the victim and in one case the defendant pleaded guilty to one charge of wilfully ill-treating the child under s 1 of the Children and Young Persons Act 1933.

Not guilty pleas

The defendant denied that they were criminally liable for the injuries to the child in six cases. In three of these cases the victim had died – one defendant pleaded not guilty to murder and two defendants pleaded not guilty to manslaughter. In two of the cases where the victim had survived the defendant pleaded not guilty to offences involving GBH. In the final case the defendant pleaded not guilty to assault occasioning ABH and the CPS offered no evidence. Therefore a contested trial took place in five cases. One defendant was convicted of manslaughter following a contested trial and three defendants were acquitted of all charges. In the one remaining case the defendant was acquitted of causing the injuries, but was convicted of neglect by failing to seek medical assistance for the child.

Sentencing

In total nine defendants were sentenced, eight having been found to have caused the injuries and one having been found guilty of neglect. Of these, seven were sentenced to an immediate custodial sentence (two fathers following convictions for manslaughter, three fathers and one mother following one or more convictions for inflicting GBH and one father following a conviction for assault). One mother convicted of inflicting GBH was placed on probation for three years and the mother convicted of neglect was given a suspended custodial sentence.

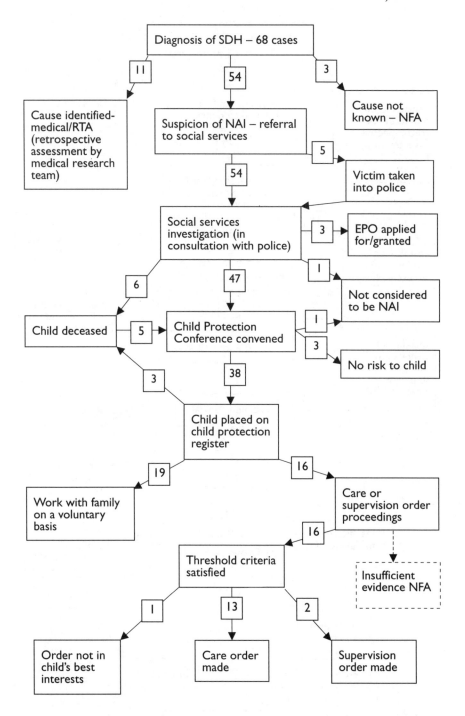

A.1: Progress of cases through the child protection system

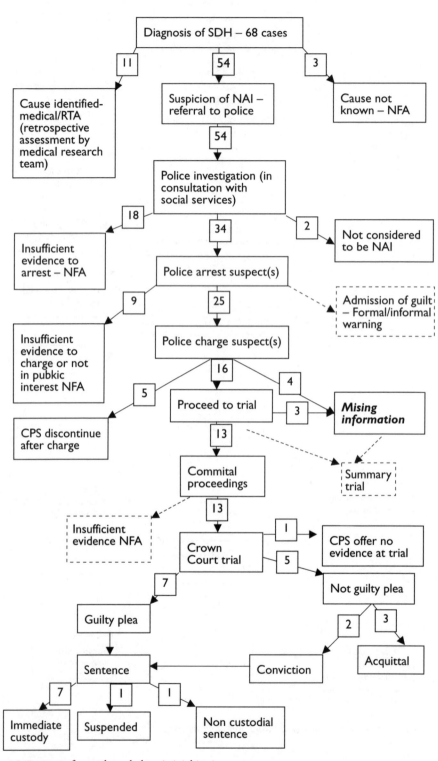

A.2: Progress of cases through the criminial justice system

References

Abbott, A. (1988) *The System of Professions: An Essay on the Division of Expert Labour.* Chicago: University of Chicago Press.

Academy of Medical Royal Colleges (2006) *Medical Expert Witnesses: Guidance from the Academy of Medical Royal Colleges.* www.aomrc.org.uk, 26 January 2006.

Allen, R.J. and Miller, J.S. (1995) 'The expert as educator: enhancing the rationality of verdicts in child sexual abuse prosecutions.' *Psychology, Public Policy & the Law 2,* 323–338.

Andronicus, M., Oates, R.K., Peat, J., Spalding, S. and Martin, H. (1998) 'Non-accidental burns in children.' *Burns 24,* 552–558.

Ards, S. and Harrell, A. (1993) 'Reporting of child maltreatment: a secondary analysis of the National Incidence Surveys.' *Child Abuse and Neglect 17,* 3, 337–344.

Arksey, H. (1994) 'Expert and lay participation in the construction of medical knowledge.' *Sociology of Health and Illness 16,* 4, 448–468.

Attorney General (2004) *The Review of Infant Death Cases.* www.lslo.gov.uk, 21 December 2004.

Attorney General (2006) *The Review of Infant Death Cases: Addendum to Report Shaken Baby Syndrome.* www.lslo.gov.uk, 14 February 2006.

Atwal, G.S., Rutty, G.N., Carter, N. and Green, M.A. (1998) 'Bruising in non-accidental head injured children: a retrospective study of the prevalence, distribution and pathological associations in 24 cases.' *Forensic Science International 96,* 215–230.

Baldwin, J.A. and Oliver, J.E. (1975) 'Epidemiology and family characteristics of severely-abused children.' *British Journal of Preventive and Social Medicine 29,* 4, 205–221.

Bandak, F. (2005) 'Shaken baby syndrome: a biomechanics analysis of injury mechanisms.' *Forensic Science International 151,* 71–79.

Barber, M.A. and Sibert, J.R. (2000) 'Diagnosing physical child abuse: the way forward.' *Postgraduate Medical Journal 76,* 743–749.

Barker, K.K. (1998) 'A ship upon a stormy sea: the medicalisation of pregnancy.' *Social Science and Medicine 47,* 8, 1067–1076.

Barlow, K.M., Thomson, E. and Minns, R.A. (1999) 'The neurological and neuropsychological outcome of non-accidental head injury.' *European Journal of Paediatric Neurology 3,* 139–141.

Barlow, K.M. and Minns, R.A. (2000) 'Annual incidence of shaken impact syndrome in young children.' *The Lancet 356,* 1571–1572.

Barton, S. (2000) 'Which clinical studies provide the best evidence?' *British Medical Journal 321,* 255–256.

Becker, J.C., Liersch, R., Tautz, C., Schlueter, B. and Andler, W. (1998) 'Shaken baby syndrome: report on four pairs of twins.' *Child Abuse & Neglect 22,* 931–937.

Benger, J.R. and McCabe, S.E. (2001) 'Burns and scalds in pre-school children attending accident and emergency: accident or abuse?' *Emergency Medicine Journal 18,* 172–174.

Best, A. and Glik, D. (2003) 'Research as a tool for integrative health service reform.' In M. Kelner, B. Wellman, B. Pescosolido and M. Saks (eds) *Complementary and Alternative Medicine: Challenge and Change.* London: Routledge.

Betchel, K., Stoessel, K., Leventhal, J.M., Ogle, E. and Teague, B. (2004) 'Characteristics that distinguish accidental from abusive injury in hospitalised young children with head trauma.' *Pediatrics 114,* 1, 165–168.

Bevan, V. and Lidstone, K. (1985) *A Guide to the Police and Criminal Evidence Act 1984.* London: Butterworths.

Blanc, R.H. and Burau, V. (2004) *Comparative Health Policy.* Houndmills: Palgrave.

Booth, P. (2005) 'The punishment of children.' *Family Law 35,* 33-35.

Borum, R. and Grisso, T. (1996) 'Establishing standards for criminal forensic reports: an empirical analysis.' *Bulletin of American Academy of Psychiatry and the Law 24,* 297–317.

Bourne, R. and Newberger, E. (eds) (1979) *Critical Perspectives on Child Abuse.* Lexington, Mass: Lexington Books.

Breslin, R. and Evans, H. (2004) *Key Child Protection Statistics: Children 'in Need'.* London: NSPCC.

Brophy, J. and Bates, P. (1999) *The Guardian ad Litem, Complex Cases and the Use of Experts following the Children Act 1989.* London: Lord Chancellor's Department.

Brosco, J.P. (2002) 'Weight charts and well child care: when the paediatrician became the expert in child health.' In A.M. Stern and H. Markel (eds) *Formative Years: Children's Health in the United States, 1880–2000.* Ann Arbor: University of Michigan Press.

Butler Sloss, E. (1988) *Report of the Inquiry into Child Abuse in Cleveland in 1987.* London: HMSO.

Caffey, J. (1972) 'On the theory and practice of shaking infants: its potential residual effects of permanent brain damage and mental retardation.' *American Journal of Diseases in Childhood 124,* 161–169.

Cartwright, S.A. (1851) 'Report on the disease and physical peculiarities of the negro race.' In A.L. Caplan, H.T. Engelhardt and J.J. McCartney (eds) *Concepts of Health and Disease: Interdisciplinary Perspectives.* New York: Addison-Wesley.

Cawson, P. (2002) *Child Maltreatment in the Family: The Experience of a National Sample of Young People.* London: NSPCC.

Cawson, P., Wattam, C., Brooker, S. and Kelly, G. (2000) *Child Maltreatment in the United Kingdom: A Study of the Prevalence of Abuse and Neglect.* London: NSPCC.

Chadwick, D.L. and Parrish, R. (2000) 'DTP vaccination or SBS? The role of irresponsible medical expert testimony in creating a false causal connection.' *SBS Quarterly,* Fall 2000. www.dontshake.com, 3 October 2006.

CIBA Foundation (1984) *Child Sexual Abuse within the Family.* London: Tavistock.

Cobley, C. (1995) *Child Abuse and the Law.* London: Cavendish Publishing.

Cobley, C. (2004) 'Working Together? – admissions of abuse in child protection proceedings and criminal prosecutions.' *Child and Family Law Quarterly 16,* 2, 175–187.

Cobley, C. and Sanders, T. (2003) 'Shaken baby syndrome: child protection issues when children sustain a subdural haemorrhage.' *Journal of Social Welfare and Family Law 25,* 2, 101–119.

Cobley, C., Sanders, T. and Wheeler, P. (2003) 'Prosecuting cases of suspected "shaken baby syndrome" – a review of current issues.' *Criminal Law Review,* February, 93–106.

Coghlan, A. (2005) 'Infant deaths: Justice for the innocents.' *New Scientist 2510,* 30 July, p.6.

Conrad, P. (1979) 'Types of medical social control.' *Sociology of Health and Illness 1,* 1, 1–11.

Conrad, P. and Schneider, J.W. (1992) *Deviance and Medicalization: From Badness to Sickness.* Philadelphia: Temple University Press.

Corby, B. (2003) 'Towards a new means of inquiry into child abuse cases.' *Journal of Social Welfare and Family Law 25,* 3, 229–241.

Creighton, S. (2004) *Prevalence and Incidence of Child Abuse: International Comparisons.* London: NSPCC.

Creighton, S. and Tissier, G. (2003) *Child Killings in England and Wales.* London: NSPCC.

Crown Prosecution Service (2004) *Code of Practice for Crown Prosecutors.* London: Crown Prosecution Service.

Crown Prosecution Service (2006) 'Disclosure: experts' evidence and unused material – guidance booklet for experts.' *Disclosure Manual, Annex K.* London: Crown Prosecution Service.

Daniel, P. and Ivatts, J. (1998) *Children and Social Policy.* London: Macmillan.

De Swaan, A. (1989) 'The reluctant imperialism of the medical profession.' *Social Science and Medicine 28,* 11, 1165–1170.

Department for Constitutional Affairs (2005) *Consultation on Proposed Rules about Expert Evidence*, Criminal Procedure Rules Committee, October 2005. London: Department for Constitutional Affairs.

Department for Education and Skills (2003) *Every Child Matters*. Cm 5860. London: Stationery Office.

Department for Education and Skills, Department of Health and Home Office (2003) *Keeping Children Safe: The Government's Response to the Victoria Climbié Inquiry Report and Joint Chief Inspector's Report Safeguarding Children*. Cm 5861. London: Stationery Office.

Department for Education and Skills (2004a) *Support from the Start*. Research Report 524. London: Department for Education and Skills.

Department for Education and Skills (2004b) *Review of Children's Cases*. Local Authority Circular (2004) 5. London: Department for Education and Skills.

Department for Education and Skills (2005a) *Inter-agency Co-operation to Improve the Well-being of Children: Children's Trusts*. London: Department for Education and Skills.

Department for Education and Skills (2005b) *Duty to Make Arrangements to Safeguard and Promote the Welfare of Children*. London: Department for Education and Skills.

Department for Education and Skills (2005c) *Guidance on the Children and Young People's Plan*. London: Department for Education and Skills.

Department for Education and Skills (2005d) *The Role and Responsibilities of the Director of Children's Services and the Lead Member for Children*. London: Department for Education and Skills.

Department for Education and Skills (2005e) *Better Services for Children as Government Acts on Lord Laming Recommendation*. Government News Network, www.gnn.gov.uk, 8 December 2005.

Department for Education and Skills (2006a) *Referrals, Assessments and Children and Young People on Child Protection Registers, England: Year Ending 31 March 2005*. London: Stationery Office.

Department for Education and Skills (2006b) *Working Together to Safeguard Children*. London: Department for Education and Skills.

Department of Health (1980) *Child Abuse: Central Register Systems*. LASSL 80(4). London: Department of Health.

Department of Health (1995) *Child Protection: Messages from Research*. London: HMSO.

Department of Health (1998) *Working Together to Safeguard Children: New Government Proposals for Inter-Agency Co-operation Consultation Paper*. London: Department of Health.

Department of Health (2000) *Framework for the Assessment of Children in Need and their Families*. London: Stationery Office.

Department of Health, Home Office and Department for Education and Employment (1999) *Working Together to Safeguard Children*. London: Stationery Office.

Department of Health, Home Office, Department for Education and Skills, Welsh Assembly (2002) *Safeguarding Children in Whom Illness is Fabricated or Induced*. London: Stationery Office.

Department of Health, Home Office, Department for Education and Skills, Department of Culture and Sport, Office of the Deputy Prime Minister, Lord Chancellor's Department (2003) *What to Do if You are Worried a Child is Being Abused: Children's Services Guidance*. London: Department of Health.

Department of Health and Social Security (1985) *Review of Child Care Law: Report to Ministers of an Interdepartmental Working Party*. London: HMSO.

Department of Health and the Welsh Office (1988) *Working Together: A Guide to Arrangements for Inter-agency Co-operation for the Protection of Children from Abuse*. London: HMSO.

Donohoe, M. (2003) 'Evidence based medicine and shaken baby syndrome. Part I: Literature review, 1966–1998.' *American Journal of Forensic Medical Pathology 24*, 239–242.

Duhaime, A.C. (1988) 'The shaken baby syndrome: a misnomer?' *Journal of Pediatric Neuroscience 4*, 77.

Duhaime, A.C., Gennarelli, T.A., Thilbault, L.E. *et al.* (1987) 'The shaken baby syndrome: a clinical, pathological, and biomechanical study.' *Journal of Neurosurgery 66*, 409–415.

Dyer, C. (2005a) '"Accuser" paediatrician can stay on register, judge rules.' *Guardian* 15 April, p.10.

Dyer, C. (2005b) '"Innocent parents at risk" in baby death cases too complex for juries' *Guardian* 7 November, p.12.

Dyer, C. (2006) 'So what happened to all the feared miscarriages of justice?' *Guardian* 9 January, p.12.

European Committee on Crime Problems (1981) *Criminological Aspects of the Ill-Treatment of Children in the Family*. Strasbourg: Council of Europe.

Evans, H.H. (2004) 'The medical discovery of shaken baby syndrome and child physical abuse.' *Pediatric Rehabilitation 7*, 3, 161–163.

Felzen, J.C. (2002) 'Child maltreatment 2002: recognition, reporting and risk.' *Pediatrics International 44*, 554–560.

Fleck, L. (1935) *Genesis and Development of a Scientific Fact*. Basel: Benno Schwabe and Co.

Foley, L. and Faircloth, C.A. (2003) 'Medicine as discursive resource: legitimation in the work narratives of midwives.' *Sociology of Health and Illness 25*, 165–184.

Friston, M. (1999) 'New rules for expert witnesses.' *British Medical Journal 318*, 1365–1366.

Frith, M. (2004) 'Child abuse review: just one case is flawed.' *Independent* 17 November, p.12.

Fung, E.L.W., Sung, R.Y.T., Nelson, E.A.S. and Poon, W.S. (2000) 'Unexplained subdural hematoma in young children: is it always child abuse?' *Pediatrics International 44*, 37–42.

Geddes, J.F. and Plunkett, J. (2004a) 'The evidence base for shaken baby syndrome.' *British Medical Journal 328*, 719–720.

Geddes, J.F. and Plunkett, J. (2004b) 'The evidence base for shaken baby syndrome: author's reply to article by Reece, R.M. (2004).' *British Medical Journal 328*, 1317.

Geddes, J.F. and Whitwell, H.L. (2004) 'Inflicted head injury in infants.' *Forensic Science International 146*, 83–88.

Geddes, J.F., Vowles, G.H., Hackshaw, A.K., Nickols, C.D., Scott, I.S. and Whitwell, H.L. (2001) 'Neuropathology of inflicted head injury in children.' *Brain 124*, 7, 1299–1306.

Geddes, J., Tasker, R., Hacksaw, A. *et al.* (2003) 'Dural haemorrhage in non-traumatic infant deaths: Does it explain the bleeding in "shaken baby syndrome?"' *Neuropathology and Applied Neurobiology 29*, 1, 14–22.

Giddens, A. (1991) *Modernity and Self Identity: Self and Society in the Late Modern Age*. Cambridge: Blackwell.

Gieryn, T.F. (1983) 'Boundary work and the demarcation of science from non-science: strains and interests in professional ideologies of scientists.' *American Sociological Review 48*, 781–795.

Gooderham, P. (2005) 'Medical Expert Witnesses at the GMC.' *Medical Law Monitor 12*, 8, 1–3.

Green, M.A. (1998) 'Shaken babies.' *The Lancet 352*, 815.

Gumpert, C.H. and Lindblad, F. (1999) 'Expert testimony on child sexual abuse: a qualitative study of the Swedish approach to statement analysis.' *Expert Evidence 7*, 279–314.

Gumpert, C.H. and Lindblad, F. (2001) 'Communication between courts and expert witnesses in legal proceedings concerning child sexual abuse in Sweden: a case review.' *Child Abuse & Neglect 25*, 1497–1516.

Haeringen, A.R.V., Dadds, M. and Armstrong, K.L. (1998) 'The child abuse lottery – will the doctor suspect and report? Physician attitudes towards and reporting of suspected child abuse and neglect.' *Child Abuse & Neglect 22*, 159–169.

Hale, B. 'In defence of the Children Act' (2000) *Archives of Disease in Childhood 83*, 463–467.

Hallet, C. and Stevenson, O. (1980) *Child Abuse: Aspects of Inter-professional Co-operation*. London: Allen & Unwin.

Halpern, S.A. (1990) 'Medicalization as professional process: postwar trends in pediatrics.' *Journal of Health and Social Behaviour 31*, 28–42.

Harrison, C., Masson, J. and Spencer, N. (2001) 'Who is failing abused and neglected children?' *Archives of Disease in Childhood 85*, 300–302.

Hawkes, N. (2006) 'Council to challenge ruling on Meadow.' *The Times*, 2 March, p.9.

Hayes, J. (2000) 'The threshold test and the unknown perpetrator.' *Family Law 30*, 260–267.

Hayes, M. (2004) 'Uncertain evidence and risk-taking in child protection cases.' *Child and Family Law Quarterly 16*, 1, 63–86.

Hayes, M. (2005) 'Criminal trials where the child is a victim: extra protection for children or a missed opportunity.' *Child and Family Law Quarterly 17*, 3, 307–327.

Hendrick, H. (2005) *Child Welfare and Social Policy.* Bristol: Policy Press.

Hobbs, C., Childs, A.M., Wynne, J., Livingston, J. and Seal, A. (2005) 'Subdural haematoma and effusion in infancy: an epidemiological study.' *Archives of Diseases in Childhood 90*, 952–955.

Holmgren, B.K. (1999) 'The legal system's role in facilitating irresponsible expert testimony.' *SBS Quarterly*, Summer 1999. www.dontshake.com, 3 October 2006.

Home Office (2005) *The Domestic Violence, Crime and Victims Act. The New Offence of Causing or Allowing the Death of a Child or Vulnerable Adult.* London: Home Office Circular 9/2005.

Home Office, Department of Health, Department of Education and Science and the Welsh Office (1991) *Working Together under the Children Act 1989.* London: HMSO.

Home Office, Ministry of Health and Ministry of Education (1950) *Children Neglected or Ill-Treated in Their Own Homes* (joint circular). London: Home Office.

Horton, R. (2005) 'A dismal and dangerous verdict against Roy Meadow.' *The Lancet 366*, 272–278.

Hosking, G. and Walsh, I. (2005) *Violence and What to Do about It: The Wave Report 2005.* Croydon: The Wave Trust.

House of Commons (2005a) 'Forensic evidence on trial.' *Select Committee on Science and Technology Seventh Report HC 96-1.* London: House of Commons.

House of Commons (2005b) 'Forensic evidence on trial.' *Government Response to the Select Committee on Science and Technology Seventh Report HC 427.* London: House of Commons.

Hunt, J. and Macleod, A. (1999) *The Best-Laid Plans: Outcomes of Judicial Decisions in Child Protection Proceedings.* London: Stationery Office.

Hymel, K. (2005) 'Small steps in the right direction: the ongoing challenge of research regarding inflicted traumatic brain injury.' *Child Abuse and Neglect 29*, 9, 945–947.

Inquiry Report (1974) *Report of the Committee of Inquiry into the Care and Supervision Provided in Relation to Maria Colwell.* London: HMSO.

Jayawant, S., Rawlinson, A., Gibbon, F. *et al.* (1998) 'Subdural haemorrhages in infants: population based study.' *British Medical Journal 317*, 1558–1561.

Jenny, C., Hymel, K.P., Ritzen, A., Reinert, S.E. and Hay, T.C. (1999) 'Analysis of missed cases of abusive head trauma.' *Journal of the American Medical Association 282*, 621–626.

Jones, C. (1994) *Expert Witnesses: Science, Medicine, and the Practice of Law.* Oxford: Clarendon Press.

Kalokerinos, A. (2005) 'Abuse or infection?' *New Scientist 2516*, 10 September, 22.

Karandikar, S., Coles, L., Jayawant, S. and Kemp, A.M. (2004) 'The neurodevelopmental outcomes in infants who have sustained a subdural haemorrhage from non-accidental head injury.' *Child Abuse Review 12*, 178–187.

Kemp, A.M. (2002) 'Investigating subdural haemorrhages in infants.' *Archives of Disease in Childhood 86*, 98–102.

Kemp, A.M., Mott, A.M. and Sibert, J.R. (1994) 'Accidents and child abuse in bathtub submersions.' *Archives of Disease in Childhood 70*, 435–438.

Kemp, A.M., Stoodley, N., Cobley, C., Coles, L. and Kemp, K.W. (2003) 'Apnoea and brain swelling in non-accidental head injury.' *Archives of Disease in Childhood 88*, 472–476.

Kempe, C.H. (1971) 'Paediatric implications of the battered baby syndrome.' *Archives of Disease in Childhood 46*, 28–37.

Kempe, C.H., Silverman, F.N., Steele, B.F., Droegemueller, W. and Silver, H.K. (1962) 'The battered child syndrome.' *Journal of the American Medical Association 181*, 17–24.

Keogh, A. (2004) 'Experts in the dock.' *New Law Journal 154*, 1762–1764.

King, W. and Reid, C. (2003) 'National audit of emergency department child protection.' *Emergency Medicine Journal 20*, 222–224.

Kleinman, P.K. (1998) 'Shaken babies.' *The Lancet 352*, 815.

Kmietowicz, Z. (2004) 'Complaints against doctors in child protection work have increased five fold.' *British Medical Journal 328*, 601–603.

Kotch, J.B., Browne, D.C. and Ringwalt, C.L. (1995) 'Risk of child abuse or neglect in a cohort of low income children.' *Child Abuse & Neglect 19*, 115–1130.

Kuhlmann, E. (2004) 'Standards, guidelines and evidence-based medicine: bringing patients' perspectives in.' *Society for the Social Studies of Science Conference*, Paris.

Laming, Lord (2003) *The Victoria Climbié Inquiry: Report of an Inquiry by Lord Laming*. Cm 5730. London: Stationery Office.

Lantz, P.E. (2004) 'The evidence base for shaken baby syndrome.' *British Medical Journal 329*, 741–742.

Lantz, P.E., Sinal, S.H., Stanton, C.A. and Weaver, R.G. (2004) 'Perimacular retinal folds from childhood head trauma: case report with critical appraisal of current literature.' *British Medical Journal 328*, 754–756.

Law Commission (2003) *Children: Their Non-accidental Death or Serious Injury (Criminal Trials)*. Law Com No 282. London: Stationery Office.

Legal Services Commission (2004) *The Use of Experts: Quality, Price and Procedures in Publicly Funded Cases*. Legal Services Commission Consultation Paper.

Lusk, A. (1996) 'Rehabilitation without acknowledgement.' *Family Law 26*, 742–745.

Lyon, C. with Cobley, C., Petrie, S. and Reid, C. (2003) *Child Abuse*. Bristol: Family Law.

Mackay, R. (1993) 'The consequences of killing very young children.' *Criminal Law Review January 1993*, 21–30.

Mahendra, B. (2005) 'Shaken by science, again.' *New Law Journal 155*, 1213–1214.

Marcovitch, H. (1999) 'Opening eyes to child abuse.' *British Medical Journal 318*, 950.

Mark, V.H. and Ervin, F.R. (1970) *Violence and the Brain*. New York: Harper and Row.

Mathew, M.O., Ramamohan, N. and Bennet, G.C. (1998) 'Importance of bruising associated with paediatric fractures: prospective observational study.' *British Medical Journal 317*, 1117–1118.

Mercier, J. (1972) 'Who is normal? Two perspectives on mild mental retardation.' In E. Jaco (ed.) *Patients, Physicians and Illness*. New York: Free Press.

Merton, D.F. and Carpenter, R.L.M. (1990) 'Radiologic imaging of inflicted injury in the child abuse syndrome.' *Pediatric Clinics of North America 37*, 815–835.

Morris, J.L., Johnson, C.F. and Clasen, M. (1985) 'To report or not to report: physicians' attitudes towards discipline and child abuse.' *American Journal of Diseases of Children 139*, 194–197.

National Assembly for Wales (2000) *Working Together to Safeguard Children*. Cardiff: Stationery Office.

National Assembly for Wales (2005) *Local Authority Child Protection Registers 2005*. Statistical Release 84/2005. Cardiff: National Assembly for Wales.

Norfolk, G.A. (1997) 'Opinions given by medical experts in court are honest and objective.' *British Medical Journal 314*, 832.

NSPCC (2001) 'Protect babies from harm.' Press release, 6 September 2001.

NSPCC (2002) 'Stop parents getting away with murder.' Press release, 1 November 2002.

NSPCC (2003) 'NSPCC and UWCM unite to educate on Shaken Baby Syndrome.' Press release, 15 January 2003.

NSPCC (2004) 'The relationship between child death and child maltreatment.' *Policy Practice Research Studies*. London: NSPCC.

Oates, K. (1982) *Child Abuse – A Community Concern*. London: Butterworths.

Ommaya, A.K. (2002) 'Biomechanics and neuropathology of adult and paediatric head injury.' *British Journal of Neurosurgery 16*, 3, 220–242.

Pamplin, C. (2004) 'Taking experts out of court.' *New Law Journal 154*, 1771–1773.

Parton, N. (1985) *The Politics of Child Abuse*. London: Macmillan.

Parton, N. (1991) *Governing the Family, Child Care, Child Protection and the State*. London: Macmillan.

Parton, N. (2004) 'From Maria Colwell to Victoria Climbié: reflections on public inquiries into child abuse a generation apart.' *Child Abuse Review 13*, 80–94.

Parton, N. (2005) *Safeguarding Childhood: Early Intervention and Surveillance in a Late Modern Society.* London: Palgrave Macmillan.

Perry, A. (2000) 'Section 31 – threshold or barrier?' *Child and Family Law Quarterly 12*, 3, 301–309.

Perry, B. (1995) 'Incubated in terror: neurodevelopment factors in the cycle of violence.' In J. Osofsky (ed.) *Children in a Violent Society.* New York: Guilford Press.

Plunkett, J. (1998) 'Shaken baby syndrome and other mysteries.' Letter submitted to the *American Journal of Forensic Medicine and Pathology,* Spring 1998, www.portia.org/ chapter08/mystery.html, 3 October 2006.

Plunkett, J. (2001) 'Fatal pediatric injuries caused by short-distance falls.' *American Journal of Forensic Medicine and Pathology 22*, 1–12.

Reder, P. and Duncan, S. (2004) 'Making the most of the Victoria Climbié Inquiry Report.' *Child Abuse Review 13*, 95–114.

Redmayne, M. (1999) 'Standards of proof in civil litigation.' *Modern Law Review 62*, 2, 167–195

Reece, R.M. (2004) 'The evidence base for shaken baby syndrome.' *British Medical Journal 328*, 1316–1317.

Richmond, J.B. (1975) 'An idea whose time has come.' *Pediatric Clinics of North America 22*, 3, 517–523.

Roberts, P. and Zuckerman, A. (2004) *Criminal Evidence.* Oxford: Oxford University Press.

Royal College of Paediatricians and Child Health (2004) *Child Protection Survey.* www.rcpch.ac.uk, 8 March 2004.

Royal College of Paediatricians and Child Health (2006) *Biggest Ever Doctor Child Protection Training Drive Launched by RCPCH and NSPCC.* www.rcpch.ac.uk, 10 January 2006.

Royal College of Pathologists and Royal College of Paediatricians and Child Health (2004) *Sudden Unexpected Death in Infancy: A Multi-agency Protocol for Care and Investigation.* www.rcpath.org, 3 October 2006.

Royal Commission on Criminal Justice (1993) *Report.* Cm 2263. London: HMSO.

Russell, M., Lazenbatt, A., Freeman, R. and Marcenes, W. (2004) 'Child physical abuse: health professionals' perceptions, diagnosis and responses.' *British Journal of Community Nursing 9*, 8, 332–338.

Sackett, D.L., Richardson, W.S., Rosenberg, W. and Haynes, R.B. (1997) *Evidence-Based Medicine.* New York: Churchill-Livingstone.

Sanders, T., Cobley, C., Coles, L. and Kemp, A. (2003) 'Factors affecting clinical referral of young children with a subdural haemorrhage to child protection agencies.' *Child Abuse Review 12*, 358–373.

Shuman, D.W., Greenberg, S., Heilbrun, K. and Foote, W.E. (1998) 'An immodest proposal: should treating mental health professionals be barred from testifying about their patients?' *Behavioral Sciences and the Law 16*, 502–523.

Sibert, J.R., Payne, E.H., Kemp, A.M. *et al.* (2002) 'The incidence of severe child abuse in Wales.' *Child Abuse and Neglect 26*, 3, 267–276.

Sidebotham, P.D. (2003) 'Red skies, risk factors and early indicators.' *Child Abuse Review 12*, 41–45.

Sidebotham, P.D. and Pearce, A.V. (1997) 'Audit of child protection procedures in accident and emergency department to identify children at risk of abuse.' *British Medical Journal 315*, 855–856.

Smith, M. (1995) 'Parental control within the family: the nature and extent of parental violence to children.' In Department of Health *Child Protection: Messages from Research.* London: Department of Health.

Smith, R. (2004) '"Hands-off Parenting?" – Towards a reform of the defence of reasonable chastisement in the UK.' *Child and Family Law Quarterly 16*, 3, 261–272.

Speight, N. and Wynne, J. (2000a) 'Is the Children Act failing severely abused and neglected children?' *Archives of Disease in Childhood 82*, 192–196.

Speight, N. and Wynne, J. (2000b) 'In defence of the Children Act: Speight and Wynne's response.' *Archives of Disease in Childhood 83*, 463–467.

Starling, S., Holden, I. and Jenny, C. (1995) 'Abusive head trauma: the relationship of perpetrators to their victims.' *Pediatrics 95*, 2, 259–262.

Sundell, K. (1997) 'Child care personnel's failure to report child maltreatment: some Swedish evidence.' *Child Abuse and Neglect 21*, 93–105.

Tardieu, A. (1860) 'Étude médico-legal sur les services et mauvais traitements exercés sur des enfants.' *Annales d'hygiène publique de médecine légale 13*, 361–398.

Thorpe, Lord Justice (2006) 'The Chief Medical Officer's Report – its context and significance.' *Family Law 36*, 16–20.

Townsend, P., Phillimore, P. and Beattie, A. (1988) *Health and Deprivation: Inequality and the North.* London: Croom Helm.

Trocmé, N., Fallon, B., MacLaurin, B. *et al.* (2005) *Canadian Incidence Study of Reported Child Abuse and Neglect – 2003: Major Findings.* Canada: Minister of Public Works and Government Services.

Twining, W.L. (1990) *Rethinking Evidence.* Oxford: Oxford University Press.

Waitzkin, H. (1983) *The Second Sickness: Contradictions of Capitalist Health Care.* London: Free Press/Macmillan.

Wall, N. (2000) *A Handbook for Expert Witnesses in Children Act Cases.* Bristol: Family Law.

Warlock, P., Stower, M. and Barber, P. (1986) 'Patterns of fractures in accidental and non-accidental injury in children: a comparative study.' *British Medical Journal 293*, 100–102.

Wheeler, P. and McDonagh, M. (2002) *A Report into the Police Investigation of Shaken Baby Murders and Assaults in the UK.* London: Home Office.

White, C. (1999) 'Some "cot deaths" are child abuse.' *British Medical Journal 318*, 147.

Whitehead, M. and Drever, F. (1999) 'Narrowing social inequalities in health? Analysis of trends in mortality among babies of lone mothers.' *British Medical Journal 318*, 1–5.

Wilczynski, A. and Morris, A. (1993) 'Parents who kill their children.' *Criminal Law Review*, January, 31–36.

Wilson, A. (2005) 'Expert testimony in the dock.' *Journal of Criminal Law 69*, 4, 330–348.

Woolcock, N. (2004) 'Judge throws out shaken baby case.' *The Times* 21 April, p.3.

Woolf, Lord (1996) *Access to Justice: Final Report.* London: Stationery Office.

Wynne, J. and Hobbs, C. (1998) 'Shaken babies.' *The Lancet 352*, 815.

Zander, M. (2000) 'The criminal standard of proof – how sure is sure?' *New Law Journal 150*, 1517–1519.

Cases

A v UK (1999) 27 EHRR 611.

A Local Authority v S and W and T [2004] EWHC 1270, [2004] 2 FLR 129.

Attorney General's Reference (No 16 of 2005) [2005] EWCA Crim 1285.

CF v Secretary of State for the Home Department [2004] EWHC 111, [2004] 2 FLR 517.

D v East Berkshire Community Health NHS Trust [2005] UKHL 23, (2005) 83 BMLR 66.

J v C [1969] 1 All ER 788.

Lancashire County Council v B [2000] 2 AC 147.

Lane v Lane (1985) 82 Cr App R 5.

Meadow v General Medical Council [2006] EWHC 146 (Admin).

North Yorkshire CC v SA [2003] EWCA Civ 839, [2003] 2 FLR 849.

R v Cannings [2004] EWCA Crim 1; [2004] 1 All ER 725.

R v Church [1966] 1 QB 59.

R v Donovan (1934) 25 Cr App R 1.

R v Doughty (1986) 83 Cr App R 319.

R v Graham (1997) 2 Cr App R (S) 264.

R v H (Assault of Child: Reasonable Chastisement) [2001] EWCA Crim 1024, [2002] 1 Cr App R 7.

R v Harris, Rock, Cherry and Faulder [2005] EWCA Crim 1980; (2005) 85 BMLR 75.

R v Hertfordshire County Council, ex parte A [2001] ELR 239.

R v Hopely (1860) 2 F & F 202.

R v Hulbert [1998] EWCA Crim 2758.

R v Kai-Whitewind [2005] EWCA Crim 1092, [2005] 2 Cr App R 31.

R v Scott (1995) 16 Cr App R (S) 451.

R v Stacey [2001] EWCA 2031, (2002) 64 BMLR 115.

R v Woollin [1999] AC 82.

Re A and D (Non Accidental Injury: Subdural Haematomas) [2002] 1 FLR 337.

Re AB (Care Proceedings: Disclosure of Medical Evidence to Police) [2002] EWHC 2198 (Fam), [2003] 1 FLR 579.

Re C (A Child) (Care Proceedings: Disclosure of Local Authority's Decision Making Process) [2002] EWHC 1379, [2002] FLR 730.

Re CB and JB (Care Proceedings: Guidelines) [1998] 2 FLR 211.

Re H (Minors) (Sexual Abuse: Standard of Proof) [1996] AC 563.

Re K (Children) (Non-Accidental Injuries; Perpetrator: New Evidence) [2004] EWCA Civ 1181, [2005] 1 FLR 285.

Re M (Care Order: Threshold Conditions) [1994] 2 FLR 577.

Re O and N (non-accidental injury): Re B (A Child) (non-accidental injury) [2003] UKHL 18, [2003] 2 All ER 305.

Re S (Sexual Abuse Allegations: Local Authority Response) [2001] EWHC Admin 334, [2001] 2 FLR 776.

Re U (A Child) (Department for Education and Skills intervening); Re B (A Child) (Department for Education and Skills intervening) [2004] EWCA Civ 567, [2005] Fam 134.

Re Y (A Child) (Split Hearing: Evidence) [2003] EWCA Civ 669, [2003] 2 FLR 273.

Re W (a child) (non-accidental injury: expert evidence) [2005] EWCA Civ 1247, [2006] 1 FLR 543.

Subject Index

Page numbers in *italics* refer to tables.

Author Index